# Accentuate the Negative

## MAKING THE MOST
## OF NEGATIVE SPACE
## IN MODERN QUILTS

Trisch Price

**Accentuate the Negative**
**Making the Most of Negative Space in Modern Quilts**
**By Trisch Price**

**Editor:** Deb Rowden
**Designer:** Sarah Mosher
**Photography:** Aaron T. Leimkuehler
**Illustration:** Eric Sears
**Technical Editor:** Jenifer Dick
**Photo Editor:** Jo Ann Groves

Published by:
Kansas City Star Books
1729 Grand Blvd.
Kansas City, Missouri, USA 64108

First edition, first printing
ISBN: 978-0-9604884-8-3

Library of Congress Control Number: 2013958005

Printed in the United States of America by Walsworth Publishing Co., Marceline, MO

To order copies, call StarInfo at (816) 234-4473.

Kansas City Star Quilts          www.mystarsblog.com

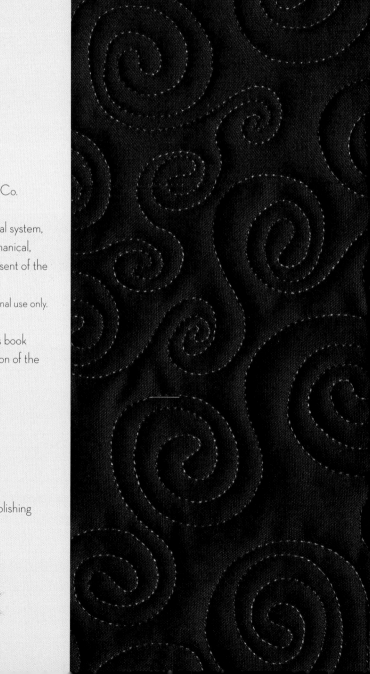

# CONTENTS

# ACKNOWLEDGEMENTS

My husband, Ray; and three children; Nick, Tyler and Kiley; for putting up with fabric and quilts all over the house, late dinners, and for general support throughout this process.

My sister, Tammy, and my mom for binding *Hopscotch* and for listening to me talk endlessly about these quilts.

Ida, Tammy, and Stephanie for giving part of themselves through their amazing quilting of *String of Pearls*, *Hopscotch*, and *Shadow Boxing*.

Mary for being my cheerleader, a great hostess, and all-around great friend.

Deb, Sarah, Aaron, Eric, Jo Ann, and Jenifer for making this process such an enjoyable experience.

My late, best-quilting-buddy Theresa, for starting me on the road to obsessive quilting!

# ABOUT THE AUTHOR

Trisch Price started quilting in the early 1990s when she was working during the day as a software engineer and attending graduate school at night. With technology seemingly taking over her life, she was in need of a low-tech diversion. Trisch started making contemporary and art quilts. Around 2005, modern quilting took over her studio.

Trisch lives in Overland Park, Kansas, with her husband and three children. She is a member of the Kansas City Modern Quilt Guild and the Blue Valley Quilters Guild. She speaks to guilds and teaches workshops. Her blog can be found at www.hadleystreetquilts.com.

# INTRODUCTION

## Going Deeper ... Growing Better

Modern Quilting is coming into its own as a movement, an aesthetic and an attitude. It began quietly, with a few talented, innovative quilters, and with the help of the internet, social media and an enthusiastic internet-savvy group of quilters, it is growing by leaps and bounds and claiming space in the quilting community.

The Modern Quilt Guild has grown alongside the movement and has organized a large group of those modern quilt enthusiasts. The excitement flourished at QuiltCon, the first national convention of The Modern Quilt Guild. Quilters who attended were inspired by what they saw and heard, and seeds were planted for the movement to grow further and faster.

As with any group that grows quickly, Modern Quilting has had growing pains and a bit of an identity crisis. Who are we? How do we define ourselves? And the big question, what is a modern quilt? There are many definitions, but those of us who self-identify as modern quilters seem to agree that there are specific aesthetic principles that tend to characterize a quilt as modern. One of those principles is how modern quilters tend to use negative space differently than traditional quilters.

This book is a result of one of those seeds planted at QuiltCon, cultivated and nourished by Trisch. She was curious and she responded by examining an aspect of modern quilts in a thoughtful, creative way, and has, through her words and example quilts, grown the movement by going deeper. She analyzed and labeled many of the ways we use negative space in our quilts and she has shown us new options for our designs.

Trisch's book, *Accentuate the Negative*, is, I hope, the first of many books that examine the characteristics of modern quilts and help us extend the conversation about modern quilting. If we dig deeper, we will learn together, and grow better.

*Jacquie Gering*

# PREFACE

The seed for this book was planted at the Modern Quilt Guild's inaugural QuiltCon show in 2013. I attended the show with several friends. For some reason unknown to me, I spent a lot of time studying the quilts in the negative space category — and examining the quilts in other categories that had great negative space. Some of the quilts had a small area of design relative to the quilt size and had lots of negative space. In others, the negative space was not an expanse of fabric, but rather interesting shapes that were formed by the positive design. Even a gradated background was represented. Some were elaborately quilted, others were simple.

When you attend a quilt show, especially for several days and especially with friends, a lot of conversations happen. You go through the show with different people and discuss varying ideas. One friend noted that she had a quilt with a lot of negative space that was beautifully quilted by a professional quilter. She didn't have any complaints about the quilting itself, as I said, it was beautiful. However, she felt that the quilt wasn't all hers because the quilting was so impactful to the design. I don't really have this problem because I quilt almost all of my quilts. But, as I thought more about it, I realized that I didn't tend to leave negative space as a completely blank slate — and the idea for this book was born!

At the end of a show, you can leave feeling intimidated, or you can leave feeling inspired. Personally, I like to leave a show feeling I have learned something that will influence my work. I'm not saying that I walk away wanting to recreate something that someone else has already made. I try to look at the body of quilts and think about where I can go from there. How does what I've seen relate to my work and my style of quilting? How I can apply that to improve and inspire my own quilts?

The next time you go to a show — or even watch show and tell — see what you can take away. When you see an awe-inspiring quilt, take a second look. Examine what it is you reacted to. Take some time to think about how you can apply this to evolve your own work.

Early in my career as a software engineer, I had a discussion with my father-in-law. He noted that you can have five years of experience or one year of experience five times. I took this to heart then, and I have always applied this to my quilting. The lesson: keep challenging yourself and try new things!

# NEGATIVE SPACE

Negative space is the space around and between prominent design elements. As quilters, we usually refer to this as the background. Traditional quilts have utilized negative space since the beginning with sashing and borders. Modern quilting has brought negative space to the forefront of design.

Negative space can be vital to a quilt design. It can add movement to a quilt. In a busy or intricate design, negative space can offer a place for the eye to rest. It can add balance to a quilt and help define boundaries.

A rule of thirds is often utilized in design — whether it's intentional or serendipitous. This is an opportunity to employ negative space.

When examining traditional quilts, the sashing between blocks often uses up the one-third. Using a little algebra, it's easy to calculate how wide a border should be in relation to a block to be one-third of the area. For a 9" block, the ideal size is 1¾"–2". For a 12" block, the ideal size is 2½". Those are both pretty typical of traditional quilts — and I'm pretty sure they weren't using algebra to figure it out. It's just a natural design aesthetic.

The rule of thirds applies beyond sashing and in modern quilts, it's more typical to see the negative space occupy two-thirds of the quilt. The aesthetic of thirds is demonstrated in the following illustration where negative space defines the boundaries of the design.

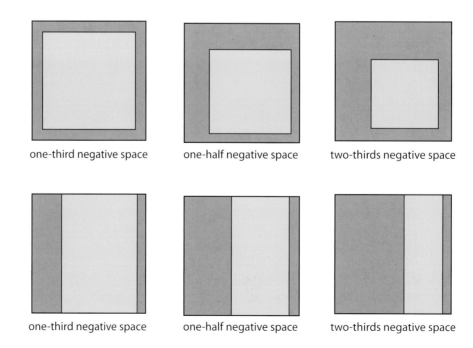

one-third negative space     one-half negative space     two-thirds negative space

one-third negative space     one-half negative space     two-thirds negative space

Often, negative space is comprised of large expanses of fabric waiting for the quilting to define it. Quilting can add movement to a quilt and further depth to a design concept. This is great, but you don't have to wait for quilting to add to the design of your quilt. If you really want to draw in a viewer, use the prominent design elements of your quilt as the first layer of design; the negative space as the second; and the quilting as the third. The more subtleties in a quilt, the more viewers are drawn in.

Negative space is a design opportunity. This space can be used to further convey the story behind a quilt. It can be used to add depth and movement to a quilt. This can all be done through fabric rather than relying solely on the quilting. The key is to keep the negative space negative and in the background. If you keep the negative space design monochromatic, with little value change, you will be successful.

In this book, six different negative space design techniques are introduced. Each chapter starts with the concept behind the technique and a general discussion of how to utilize the technique in design. Three quilts are presented in each chapter to further demonstrate the technique.

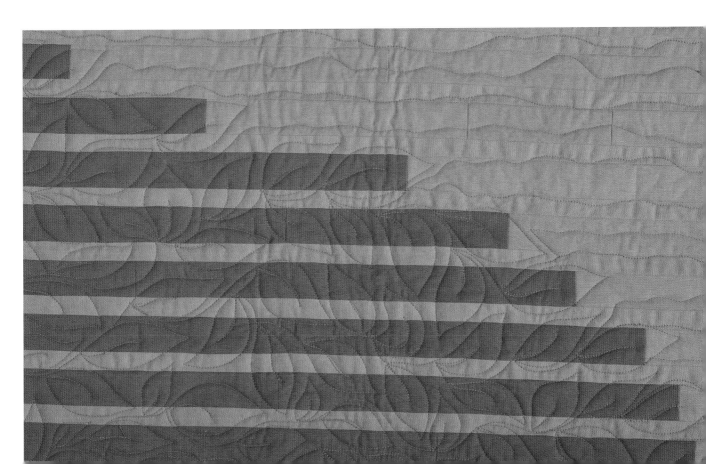

# GENERAL INSTRUCTIONS

All of the piecing in this book uses 1/4" seam allowances, unless otherwise stated.

Fat quarters measure 18" x 20".

Fat eighths measure 9" x 20".

Unless otherwise noted, all measurements are width x height.

Some of the patterns utilize **partial seaming**. This may be intimidating at first, but just dive in. It will be a habit in no time. It is a very useful technique that will allow you to expand your design possibilities. Partial seaming is most useful when you have multiple T-intersections coming together in opposing directions. To complete the seams, start with the end of one seam and stitch the last few inches. Press just the stitched end of the seam. Continue adding the remaining pieces in a traditional manner. Go back to the start and complete the seam.

## ORGANIZING CUT STRIPS

Several quilts in this book require you to cut many strips of fabric in varying lengths. The trick is to keep it all organized. Here are three methods that I use.

1. I mark each piece as I go. I do this in one of two ways. Sometimes, I use a chalk pencil and write the length on the back. Other times, I use dot stickers. If using a sticker, I first write each size I need on a sticker. Then I just take the stickers to my cutting table and follow those sizes (rather than referring to the pattern) to complete the cutting, applying the stickers as I cut.

2. Cut everything and stack it according to size. Then when I lay it out on the design wall, I can find the size I need fairly quickly. I do take the time to check the length of each piece before I add it to the design wall.

3. Cut the fabric according to the assembly diagram. I cut the piece, and immediately place it on the design wall. If I'm not cutting near my design wall, I just stack them in the same order as the diagram.

13

# GRADATION

You can add a lot of movement and depth to a quilt by using fabric gradations. This doesn't mean that you have to go out and learn how to gradation dye or hunt around for ombré fabrics. With so many solid fabrics available, it's pretty easy to put together a set of gradations.

To incorporate gradation effectively, plan an overall gradation scheme. Gradations can be used to add depth in two ways: shading and stacking.

In **shading**, fabrics are used side by side gently fading from one shade to the next with the shades being pretty close to each other. Generally speaking, lighter colors will appear closer and darker colors will move away. You can also use shading to give the quilt a light source (remember middle school art class!).

For an **overall gradated design**, as in *Boxed In* (page 16) and *Confetti Drop* (page 28), the quilt is based on two designs. The first design is the piecing of the quilt. The second is the gradation. To do this, I start with graph paper. I determine the layout of the piecing and size of the quilt. Then I start with a blank sheet that denotes the perimeter of the quilt. I determine where I want the light source, and draw radiating lines from that point to divide the quilt into areas of gradation. Overlay the designs, and determine block by block which area they fall into. When a block crosses an area, it goes to the largest part of the block.

If going for a **stacked** effect, the darker colors will give the appearance of being shadowed. The steps between the gradations should be farther apart than in shading. Stacking is most effective if there is a definite line between the design elements and can be further reinforced if the design elements are cut off as they are conceptually stacked. For a stacked effect, such as *Petrified Wood* (page 20), I use darker background to give a shadowing effect. To get the layered effect, the design elements are cut off where they would appear to be covered by a 'higher' block.

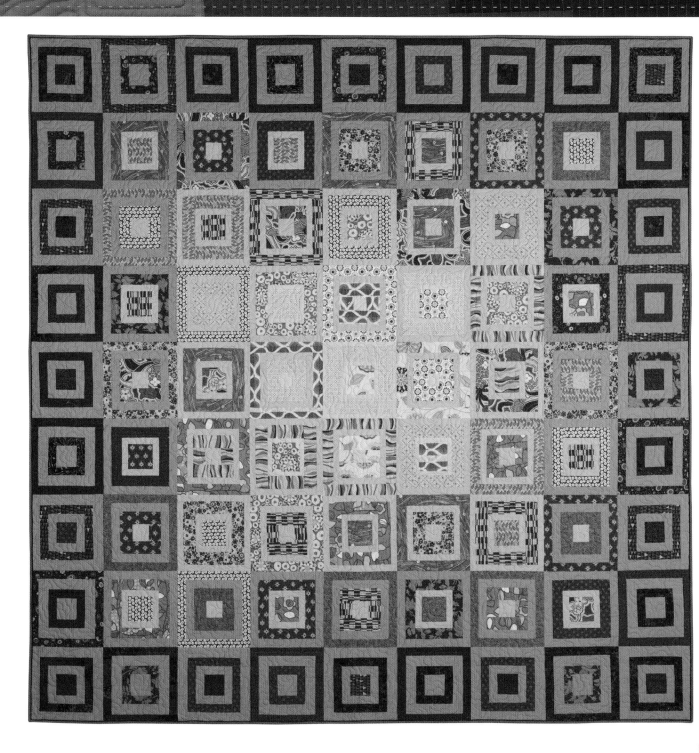

This is a simple quilt based on the traditional Courthouse Steps block. The light source is centered on the quilt and radiates out. Determining the fabric placement on this quilt is simple. Three shades are used and the shades change by row. The prints are divided by value — light, medium, and dark. To make the transitions between shades more subtle, the same prints are mixed into the adjacent areas. So, the outer rows have a dark solid and dark prints. The next row in uses the same dark solid, but the prints are darks and mediums. The size of the strips change from area to area as well. The solids are smaller in the light area and get larger as the blocks get darker. This helps to further define the gradation.

### *Boxed In* Fabric Details

I collected the pink and orange fabrics during the annual Kansas City Shop Hop a few years ago. My mom and one of my sisters come to town for the shop hop every year. This particular year, my sister and I agreed to collect pink and orange fabrics. We each bought half-yards of fabric and then split them all into fat quarters. It was a great way to get a diverse collection of fabric. The solids are Kona cottons: sand, tan, and stone. When I bought them, Konas weren't readily available and it was the best gradation in browns that I could find — there's a much better selection out there now.

## FABRIC REQUIREMENTS

### PRINTS
6 fat quarters of light prints
10 fat quarters of medium prints
10 fat quarters of dark prints

### SOLIDS
¼ yard light solid
1⅛ yards medium solid
2¼ yards dark solid

## CUTTING

### LIGHT SOLID
4 strips cut 1" x width of fabric (wof)
4 — 2" squares

### MEDIUM SOLID
27 strips cut 1¼" x wof
Cut 2 — 2½" strips
Crosscut 20 — 2½" squares.

### DARK SOLID
49 strips cut 1½" x wof
Cut 2 — 3" strips
Crosscut 16 — 3" squares.

### PRINTS
Cut strips across the short side of the fabric so the width of the fabric is approximately 18".

## 2 LIGHTEST PRINTS
### BLOCK 1
1 — 4" square
2 — 2¼" strips of the print not used for the square

## ALL LIGHT PRINTS
(INCLUDING THE 2 LIGHTEST FROM ABOVE)
### BLOCK 2
4 — 4" squares
8 — 2" strips cut in pairs from 4 different prints

### BLOCK 3
8 — 1¾" strips cut in pairs from 4 different prints
4 — 2¼" strips from 4 different prints

## MIX OF MEDIUM AND LIGHT PRINTS
(MORE MEDIUM THAN LIGHT)
### BLOCK 4
8 — 3½" squares
16 — 2" strips cut in pairs

### BLOCK 5
16 — 1¾" strips cut in pairs
8 — 2" strips from different prints
   (doesn't have to be paired)

## MEDIUM PRINTS WITH A FEW DARKS
### BLOCK 6
12 — 3½" squares
24 — 1¾" strips cut in pairs

### BLOCK 7
24 — 1½" strips cut in pairs
12 — 2" strips from different prints
   (doesn't have to be paired)

## DARK PRINTS WITH A FEW MEDIUMS
### BLOCK 8
16 — 3" squares
32 — 1¾" strips cut in pairs

### BLOCK 9
32 — 1½" strips cut in pairs
16 — 1¾" strips from different prints
   (doesn't have to be paired)

## PIECING

All of the blocks are pieced in the same manner. Start with the center block. Attach the strip for the first ring to each side. Press seams toward the print. Attach the same strip to the top and bottom, press to the print. Repeat until you have a center square surrounded by 3 rings. The block measures 9½" unfinished.

## BLOCK 1
### Make 1
Center square: 4" square of the lightest print
First ring: 1" light solid strip
Second ring: 2¼" lightest print strip
Third ring: 1" light solid strip

## BLOCK 2
### Make 4
Center square: 4" square of the light print
First ring: 1" light solid strip
Second ring: 2" light print strip
Third ring: 1¼" medium solid strip

## BLOCK 3
### Make 4
Center square: 2" square of the light solid
First ring: 2¼" light print strip
Second ring: 1¼" medium solid strip
Third ring: 1¾" light print strip

## BLOCK 4
### Make 8
Center square: 3½" square of the medium to light print
First ring: 1¼" medium solid strip
Second ring: 2" medium to light print strip
Third ring: 1¼" medium solid strip

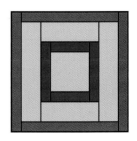

## BLOCK 5
### Make 8

Center square: 2½" square of the medium solid

First ring: 2" medium to light print strip

Second ring: 1¼" medium solid strip

Third ring: 1¾" medium to light print strip

## BLOCK 6
### Make 12

Center square: 3½" square of the medium to dark print

First ring: 1¼" medium solid strip

Second ring: 1¾" medium to dark print strip

Third ring: 1½" dark solid strip

## BLOCK 7
### Make 12

Center square: 2½" square of the medium solid

First ring: 2" medium to dark print strip

Second ring: 1½" dark solid strip

Third ring: 1½" medium to dark print strip

## BLOCK 8
### Make 16

Center square: 3" square of the dark to medium print

First ring: 1½" dark solid strip

Second ring: 1¾" dark to medium print strip

Third ring: 1½" dark solid strip

## BLOCK 9
### Make 16

Center square: 3" square of the dark solid

First ring: 1¾" dark to medium print strip

Second ring: 1½" dark solid strip

Third ring: 1½" dark to medium print strip

## ASSEMBLY

Lay out the blocks following the diagram. Sew the blocks together into rows. Sew the rows together. If you press all of the seams toward the print, they will all oppose each other and matching the seams will be easier.

| 8 | 9 | 8 | 9 | 8 | 9 | 8 | 9 | 8 |
|---|---|---|---|---|---|---|---|---|
| 9 | 6 | 7 | 6 | 7 | 6 | 7 | 6 | 9 |
| 8 | 7 | 4 | 5 | 4 | 5 | 4 | 7 | 8 |
| 9 | 6 | 5 | 3 | 2 | 3 | 5 | 6 | 9 |
| 8 | 7 | 4 | 2 | 1 | 2 | 4 | 7 | 8 |
| 9 | 6 | 5 | 3 | 2 | 3 | 5 | 6 | 9 |
| 8 | 7 | 4 | 5 | 4 | 5 | 4 | 7 | 8 |
| 9 | 6 | 7 | 6 | 7 | 6 | 7 | 6 | 9 |
| 8 | 9 | 8 | 9 | 8 | 9 | 8 | 9 | 8 |

ASSEMBLY DIAGRAM —
NUMBERS INDICATE BLOCK NUMBERS

*Petrified Wood* utilizes a stacking technique. Generally speaking, darker colors come forward in a design. However, logic tells us that objects that are in shadow are darker than those that are shading them. So, by adding definitive lines and overlaps, the shadowed areas are defined and the darker fabrics appear farther away. If you want to further define the layering, you could not only make the backgrounds gradate, you could include the foregrounds as well (using darker foreground fabrics as the backgrounds get darker). I didn't choose to do that, but it would add even more drama to the quilt.

This is a "quilt as you go" quilt. On the plus side, that means the quilting is easy because you are not working with an entire quilt top. It also results in a great quilt back. In the instructions, I use 3 different fabrics for the back; you can easily change it to six for an even more interesting back. On the down side, "quilt as you go" means that you'll be doing some hand stitching at the end. I don't use this method often, but for this quilt, I think it pays off.

Another anomaly of this quilt is the binding. I almost always use a ¼" finished binding. However, for this quilt, the binding is finished at ¾" to make it consistent with the other lines in the quilt. I think it is effective — it would look odd with a smaller binding. This means that your binding will need to be cut larger (I use the double-fold technique and cut 4¾" wide strips) and attached with a ¾" seam allowance.

*Petrified Wood*
Fabric Details
. . . . . . . . . . . . . . . . .

All of the fabrics are Kona cottons. I used three shades in the brown/cream family. The binding and sashing is Kona espresso. When selecting the colors, I kept in mind the colors found in petrified wood and the Painted Desert — only exaggerated.

## FABRIC REQUIREMENTS
. . . . . . . . . . . . . . . . . . . . . . . . . . .

### BACKGROUNDS
1½ yards light neutral
1 yard medium neutral
1½ yards dark neutral

### SASHING AND BINDING
1½ yards dark brown

### ASSORTED COLORS
¾ yard of 6 different colors
Scraps to ½ yard in a variety of colors

### BACKING
1½ yards print 1
1 yard print 2
1½ yards print 3

## SUPPLIES
. . . . . . . . . . . . . . .

Starch
¾" bias tape maker
Twin size batting

# Petrified Wood

## CUTTING

### LIGHT NEUTRAL AND BACKING PRINT 1
1 — 29" x 29"
1 — 20" x 20"
2 — 11" x 11"

### MEDIUM NEUTRAL AND BACKING PRINT 2
1 — 29" x 29"

### DARK NEUTRAL AND BACKING PRINT 3
1 — 29" x 29"
1 — 20" x 20"

### DARK BROWN
13 strips 1¼" x wof (to cover seams)
6 strips 4¾" x wof for wide binding

### COLORS
Cutting instructions are in the piecing section.

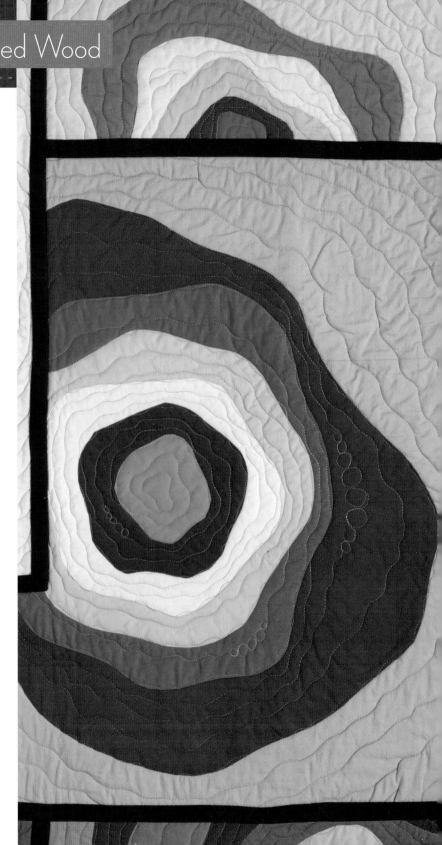

## PIECING

Start making the concentric circles for one large background piece. Begin with a piece of fabric about 6" square. Place it on your cutting surface and with a rotary cutter, cut a wonky-edged circle. Put it face down on the ironing board. Spray the outer edge with starch (it doesn't have to be exact, just so the outer ¾" is starched). Gently turn under the edges, pressing as you go until the edge of the circle is completely turned under and pressed, avoiding pleats.

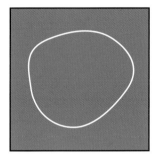

Place a larger piece of fabric on the cutting surface. Place the circle that you just finished on top. Cut the next circle so that once the edge is turned under, it is larger than the first circle. Fold and press the outer edges just like the last circle. With both pieces facing up, place the first circle on top of the second and stitch it down. To do this, you can machine appliqué using: a shortened

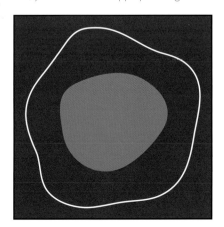

blind hem stitch; a small zigzag; topstitching; or hand appliqué. This project is not suitable for using any type of fusible. Once the first circle is attached, turn it over and trim out the portion of the larger circle that lies under the small circle.

Continue this process until you have built up enough circles to fill the background piece, leaving at least a 2" margin all the way around.

Repeat this process for all of the background squares except for 1 of the small 11" x 11" light neutral squares. Make sure you vary the color positions from block to block.

For the remaining small 11" x 11" light neutral square, the process is the same, except instead of cutting circles, cut a quarter circle and place it on 1 corner of the block. The finished block should appear to be cut from a larger piece.

Once all the background squares are filled, sandwich them with batting and backing. Quilt them individually.

## ASSEMBLY

After quilting, trim the squares. Trim the largest squares to 27", the medium squares to 18", and the small squares to 9".

Next, cut the finished squares as follows. Be careful — cut a clean line and try not to cut beyond the cutting line.

- Cut the light 18" square in half.

- Cut the medium 27" square by removing a 9" x 18" corner. (Save this corner piece.)

- Cut the dark 27" square by removing a 9" x 18" corner. (Save this corner piece.)

- Cut the dark 18" square by removing a 9" x 9" corner. (This corner piece will not be used.)

Stay stitch around each block to keep the quilting from coming loose.

Arrange all of the squares as shown on the next page — the numbers indicate the order for applying binding to cover the edges. Place the edges up against each other and with a wide zigzag, stitch the blocks together.

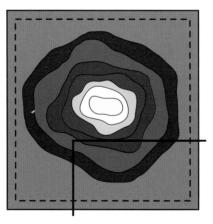
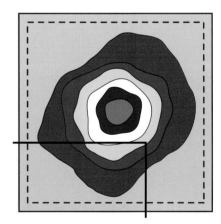

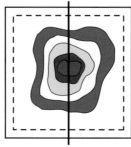
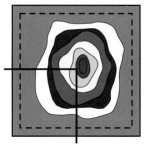

ASSEMBLY DIAGRAM

## FINISHING

Connect the 1¼" dark brown strips by sewing them together at a 45° angle. Press the seams open, then trim the excess fabric.

Using a hot iron, a bias tape maker and starch, make binding to cover the seams. Cut 1 end of the fabric at a sharp angle to make it easier to feed into the bias tape maker. Spray the wrong side of the fabric with starch, about 1 yard at a time. Feed the fabric into the bias tape maker. Once a fold comes through, place the iron on top of the fold up against the tape maker. Gently push the tape maker onto the fabric with the nose of the iron while using your other hand to guide the fabric into the tape maker. At the end of the starched area, move everything down to where you started and repeat the process until all of the fabric is folded.

Cover the seams on the quilt front with this fabric tape, using the appliqué method of your choice. Use the diagram below for placement order. Repeat the process on the back of the quilt.

To keep a consistent look, the binding is wider than usual so it is the same size as the strips that cover the seam lines in the quilt. Attach it with a ¾" seam allowance. Miter the corners by forming the corner and folding the extra under, distributing the bulk to each side of the seam.

# Confetti Drop

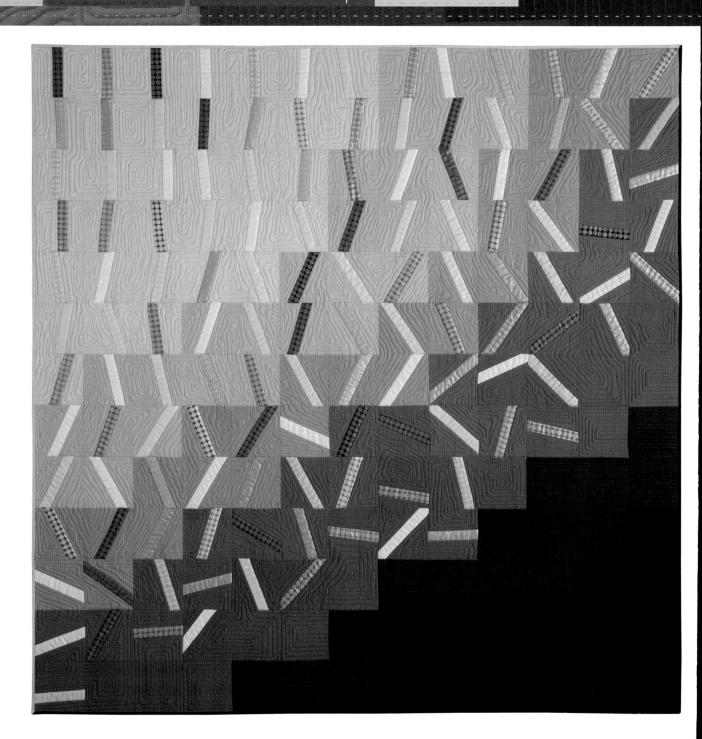

Gradated designs are effective when foreground designs change independently of the background gradation. I kept this in mind when designing *Confetti Drop*. The pieces of confetti fall from the upper left corner of the quilt. The lines start completely vertical and centered in the block. As they move away, the lines become off-centered, then at slight angles, and continue to change until they are at all angles. First, I determined where I wanted the line changes to occur. Confetti isn't going to stay straight for long! So they quickly start to change. To really get the effect of falling, I made the angles more extreme the further they had fallen.

Separate from this, I decided where the light source would be. Then I just penciled in radiating lines to define six areas. Next, I went block by block and determined to which area they belonged. If a block crossed into another area, it went to the area that had the majority of the block. I think using this method makes gradating very straightforward, and you are not struggling with the decision of which block should be in which area.

To maintain the integrity of the design, I used 2 values of gray in the binding. Across the top and down the left side, the binding is the lightest gray. Across the bottom and the right, I used the darkest.

## *Confetti Drop*
### Fabric Details

All of the solids are Kona cottons: ash, iron, medium grey, steel, coal, charcoal, and pepper. The confetti is made of various colors of Michael Miller's Mirror Ball Dot.

## FABRIC REQUIREMENTS

### BACKGROUND
Seven shades of gray — lightest being gray 1, darkest being gray 7
- 1¼ yards gray #1
- 1 yard gray #2
- 1 yard gray #3
- 1 yard gray #4
- ⅞ yard gray #5
- ⅔ yard gray #6
- ⅔ yard gray #7

### PRINTS
13–15 scraps in a variety of bright colors totaling 1⅛ yards

# Confetti Drop

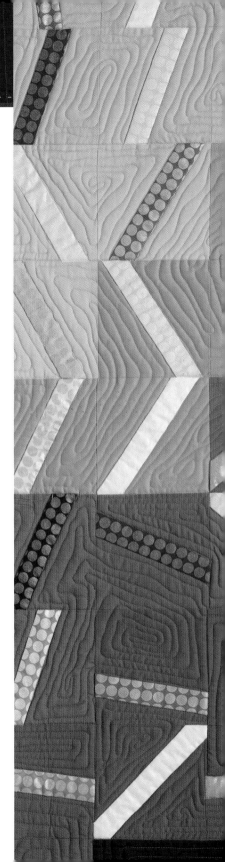

## CUTTING

### GRAY #1
Cut 6 — 6" strips x wof
Crosscut 35 — 6" squares.

### GRAY #2
Cut 5 — 6" strips x wof
Crosscut 28 — 6" squares.

### GRAY #3
Cut 5 — 6" strips x wof
Crosscut 27 — 6" squares.

### GRAY #4
Cut 5 — 6" strips x wof
Crosscut 25 — 6" squares.

### GRAY #5
Cut 3 — 6" strips x wof
Crosscut 13 — 6" squares.
Cut 2 — 5½" strips x wof
Crosscut 4 — 5½" squares.
Crosscut 2 — 5½" x 10½" rectangles.
Crosscut 1 — 5½" x 15½" rectangle.

### GRAY #6
Cut 3 — 5½" strips x wof
Crosscut 1 — 5½" square.
Crosscut 4 — 5½" x 15½" rectangles.
Crosscut 1 — 5½" x 20½" rectangle.

### GRAY #7
Cut 2 — 5½" strips x wof
Crosscut 1 — 5½" square.
Crosscut 1 — 5½" x 10½" rectangle.
Crosscut 1 — 5½" x 20½" rectangle.
Crosscut 1 — 5½" x 30½" rectangle.

### PRINTS
From the bright scrap fabric, cut strips
1½" x 8".

# PIECING

**Centered, vertical lines:** Cut the squares in half vertically. Insert a 1½" strip in each. Press. Trim to 5½", keeping the line centered and vertical.

Do this with:

- Gray #1 — 5 squares

**Vertical lines:** Cut the squares vertically, but not down the center. Insert a 1½" strip in each. Press. Trim to 5½", keeping the line vertical and NOT centered.

Do this with:

- Gray #1 – 6 squares

**Angle 1:** Cut the squares a little slanted, but mostly vertical. Insert a 1½" strip in each. Press. Trim to 5½".

Do this with:

- Gray #1 — 19 squares
- Gray #2 — 4 squares

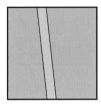

**Angle 2:** Cut the squares more slanted, but not very close to the corners. Insert a 1½" strip in each. Press. Trim to 5½".

Do this with:

- Gray #1 — 5 squares
- Gray #2 — 18 squares
- Gray #3 — 5 squares

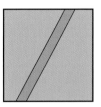

**Angle 3:** Cut the squares more slanted, close to or even across the corners. Insert a 1½" strip in each. Press. Trim to 5½".

Do this with:

- Gray #2 — 6 squares
- Gray #3 — 22 squares
- Gray #4 — 9 squares

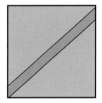

**Angle 4:** Cut the squares at near horizontal angles or angles that cut across a corner. Insert a 1½" strip in each. Press. Trim to 5½".

Do this with:

- Gray #4 — 16 squares
- Gray #5 — 13 squares

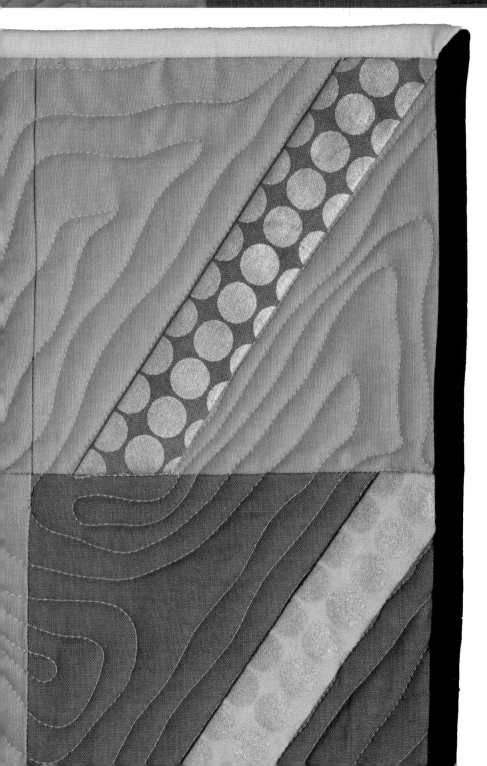

## ASSEMBLY

Lay out the quilt according to the diagram. Piece the rows. Press.

Attach the rows to finish the quilt.

| | | | | | | | | | | | | |
|---|---|---|---|---|---|---|---|---|---|---|---|---|
| G1 Cntr | G1 Cntr | G1 Cntr | G1 Cntr | G1 Cntr | G1 Ang 1 | G1 Ang 1 | G2 Ang 1 | G2 Ang 1 | G2 Ang 2 | G3 Ang 2 | G3 Ang 2 | G3 Ang 3 |
| G1 Vert | G1 Vert | G1 Vert | G1 Ang 1 | G1 Ang 1 | G1 Ang 1 | G1 Ang 1 | G2 Ang 1 | G2 Ang 2 | G2 Ang 2 | G3 Ang 2 | G3 Ang 3 | G4 Ang 3 |
| G1 Vert | G1 Vert | G1 Ang 1 | G1 Ang 1 | G1 Ang 1 | G1 Ang 1 | G2 Ang 1 | G2 Ang 2 | G2 Ang 2 | G3 Ang 2 | G3 Ang 3 | G4 Ang 3 | G4 Ang 4 |
| G1 Vert | G1 Ang 1 | G1 Ang 1 | G1 Ang 1 | G1 Ang 1 | G1 Ang 2 | G2 Ang 2 | G2 Ang 2 | G2 Ang 2 | G3 Ang 3 | G3 Ang 3 | G4 Ang 4 | G4 Ang 4 |
| G1 Ang 1 | G1 Ang 1 | G1 Ang 1 | G1 Ang 1 | G1 Ang 2 | G2 Ang 2 | G2 Ang 3 | G2 Ang 3 | G3 Ang 3 | G3 Ang 3 | G4 Ang 4 | G4 Ang 4 | G5 Ang 4 |
| G1 Ang 1 | G1 Ang 2 | G1 Ang 2 | G2 Ang 2 | G2 Ang 2 | G2 Ang 2 | G2 Ang 3 | G3 Ang 3 | G3 Ang 3 | G4 Ang 4 | G4 Ang 4 | G5 Ang 4 | G5 5 ½" |
| G1 Ang 2 | G2 Ang 2 | G2 Ang 2 | G2 Ang 2 | G2 Ang 2 | G3 Ang 2 | G3 Ang 3 | G3 Ang 3 | G4 Ang 4 | G4 Ang 4 | G5 Ang 4 | G5 10 ½" | |
| G2 Ang 2 | G2 Ang 2 | G2 Ang 3 | G3 Ang 3 | G3 Ang 3 | G3 Ang 3 | G4 Ang 3 | G4 Ang 3 | G4 Ang 4 | G5 Ang 4 | G5 Ang 4 | G5 5 ½" | G6 5 ½" |
| G2 Ang 3 | G2 Ang 3 | G3 Ang 3 | G3 Ang 3 | G3 Ang 3 | G4 Ang 3 | G4 Ang 3 | G5 Ang 4 | G5 Ang 4 | G5 5 ½" | G6 15 ½" | | |
| G3 Ang 3 | G3 Ang 3 | G3 Ang 3 | G4 Ang 3 | G4 Ang 3 | G4 Ang 4 | G5 Ang 4 | G5 Ang 4 | G5 Ang 4 | G6 15 ½" | | | G7 5 ½" |
| G3 Ang 3 | G3 Ang 3 | G4 Ang 3 | G4 Ang 4 | G5 Ang 4 | G5 Ang 4 | G5 5 ½" | G6 20 ½" | | | | G7 10 ½" | |
| G4 Ang 4 | G4 Ang 4 | G4 Ang 4 | G5 Ang 4 | G5 10 ½" | | G6 15 ½" | | | G7 20 ½" | | | |
| G4 Ang 4 | G5 15 ½" | | | G6 15 ½" | | | | G7 30 ½" | | | | |

ASSEMBLY DIAGRAM

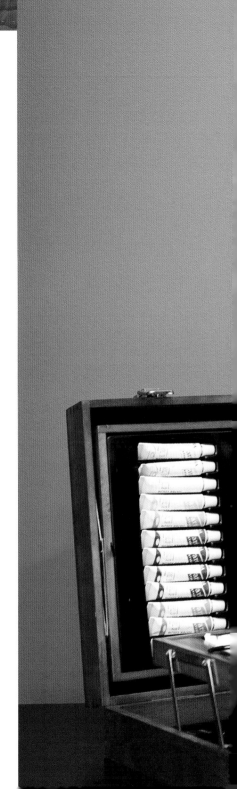

# REVERSAL

A reversal design transposes what would logically be the negative and positive spaces. The quilts in this chapter are first designed around what would logically be the positive space. In *Unchurned* (page 36), the design is an oversized, traditional Churn Dash block. In *Pencil Box* (page 40), the design is a set of simple pencils. In *Aware* (page 44), the design is an awareness ribbon. For each of these quilts, the logical background was pieced in some fashion and the prominent design element was left as a solid negative space. This is an interesting technique because your eye is initially drawn to the piecing. Upon further inspection — usually from a farther distance — the shapes made by the negative space will appear. I love to watch people when they see these quilts for the first time, especially in a more intimate setting where they are not viewing it from a distance. It always takes them a while to see the design as an entirety.

For each of these quilts, the major design elements were determined first. Then the piecing was determined to fill in what would normally be the negative space.

# Unchurned

SIZE: 72" X 72"

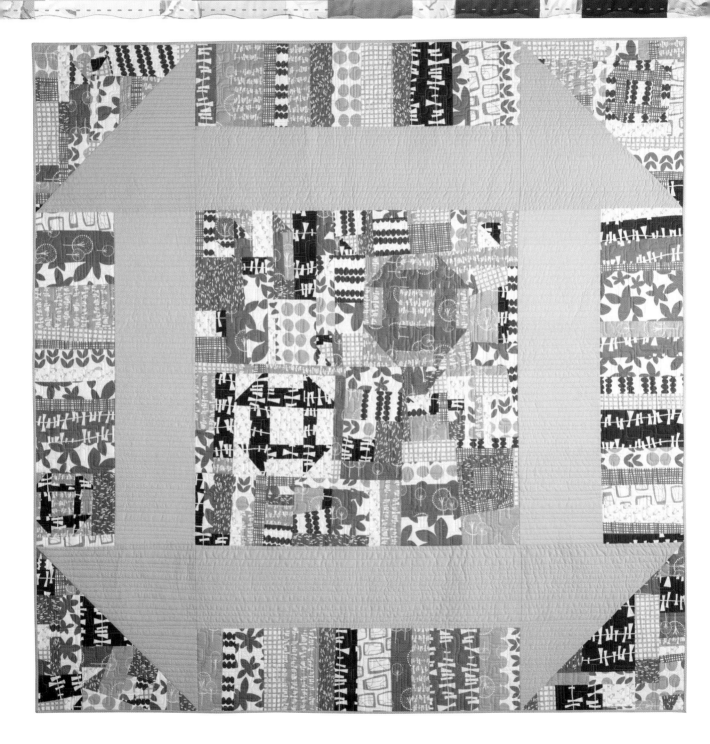

The positive space in this quilt is improvisationally pieced. It includes a few improv Churn Dash blocks embedded in the piecing. If you do not enjoy improv piecing, you can make this more traditional without degrading the overall design. Avoid using the same fabric in both the negative and positive space because it would lessen the impact of the primary design element (the large churn dash). In this quilt, I appreciate the juxtaposition of the chaotic improv piecing lines next to the long, perfectly straight lines of the oversized Churn Dash.

### *Unchurned* Fabric Details

The solid is Kona ash. The prints are from various Lotta Jansdotter collections.

## FABRIC REQUIREMENTS

1¾ yards light gray
Total of 3½ yards of varying fabrics (13–15). It's convenient to have these cut in 10" or wider strips.

## CUTTING

### GRAY

4 rectangles 9½" x 36½"
4 — 18⅞" squares. Cut each in half on the diagonal from corner to corner.

### PRINTS

For the improv churn dash blocks, cut pairs of varying fabric:

- 3 sets: 5 squares 3"
- 1 set: 5 squares 4½"
- 1 set: 5 squares 5½"

## PIECING

### SMALL IMPROV CHURN DASH BLOCKS

For each set, pair up 2 squares, right sides facing. Stitch 2 nearly parallel lines about ½" apart going down the center of the squares. The lines should be straight, but not parallel to the side of the fabric. Cut on the dashed line as shown. Press open. Make 4.

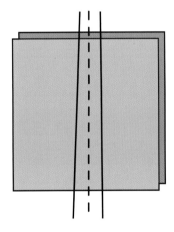

Repeat, but this time, make the lines diagonally across the square. The lines don't have to match the corners of the squares. Cut apart on the dashed line. Press open. Make 4 units.

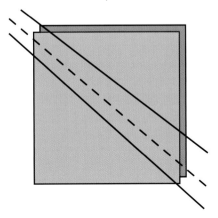

Lay out the block, using 1 of the leftover squares for the center. The extra square can be used in the improvisational piecing that follows. Piece each row together, press. Stitch the rows to each other. Press. Trim the sides so they are straight (but not square).

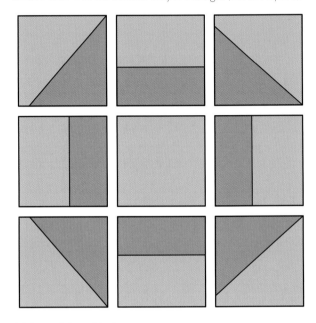

Make 5 of these blocks

## IMPROV BACKGROUND

### CENTER AND CORNER TRIANGLES

Make some extra half-square triangle blocks to sprinkle in the improvisational piecing. Cut 8 pairs of 3" squares. Put the pairs right sides together, press. Just like before, stitch 2 parallel lines ½" apart, diagonally across the squares. Cut between the 2 lines and press open.

If not using scraps, cut short (about 10") strips into a variety of widths. Using the Churn Dash blocks as a start, improvisationally piece to make a 36½" square and 2 — 18⅞" squares.

## OUTER RECTANGLES

Cut a lot of strips 10" long in a variety of widths. Piece them edge to edge until you get 4 rectangles 9½" x 36½". If you want, place a churn dash block in 1 of the rectangles. Just add fabric to the sides to get it to 10" wide. Add fabrics to either side.

## ASSEMBLY

To piece the large churn dash, match up the solid gray half-square triangle with the each improv corner triangle, right sides facing. Stitch diagonally from corner to corner. Press with the seam toward the solid gray.

Match up the solid gray rectangles with each improv rectangle. Stitch along 1 long side of each set. Press the seam toward the solid gray. Stitch the sections together as shown below.

### Improv Tips

If you notice that 1 or 2 fabrics are starting to dominate the piece (in a way that is not pleasing to you), just take those fabrics out of the scrap pile until it levels out.

When piecing, match seams occasionally. It will make the overall piecing appear more complex.

Sew straight lines — not square, but straight. When you press the seam, you want a clean edge. If the line is wavy or curved, the fabric will pleat. It may not look too bad as you piece, but it will probably show more when it's quilted.

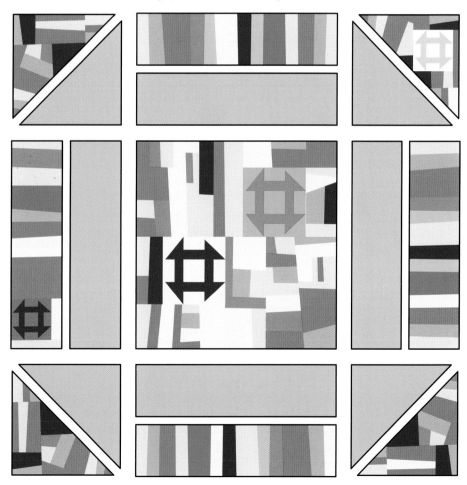

**ASSEMBLY DIAGRAM**

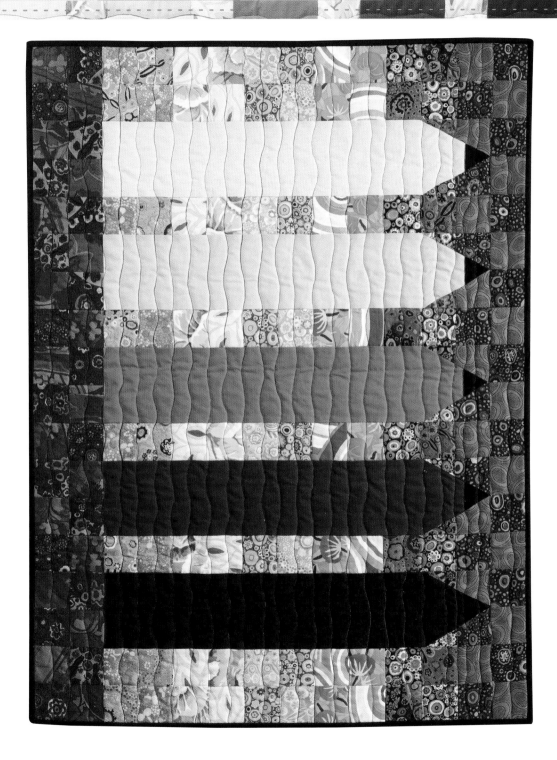

The prominent design feature of this quilt is reversal, however gradation is also employed. The positive space is simply pieced with squares that cover the range of hues (remember Roy G. Biv!). The piecing evokes the idea of an artist's palette, and the pencils represent the tools.

### *Pencil Box* Fabric Details

The solids are Kona cottons in varying shades of grey and black. The prints are from my collection of Kaffe Fassett fabrics. The background colors follow the colors of the rainbow (Roy G. Biv): red, orange, yellow, green, blue, indigo, and violet.

## FABRIC REQUIREMENTS

¼ yard of 5 shades of gray solid that gradate from light to dark.
Fat eighths of:

- 2 red prints
- 2 orange prints
- 2 yellow prints
- 2 green prints
- 2 blue prints
- 2 indigo (or blue-violet) prints
- 2 violet (on the red side) prints

Black scraps

## CUTTING

### GRAYS

Cut a 4½" x 22½" rectangle from each of the 5 gray fabrics.

### BLACK

Cut 5 — 2" squares.

### ORANGES, YELLOWS, GREENS, BLUES

From each fabric, cut 1 — 2½" strip from each fabric across the length.

### INDIGOS AND VIOLETS

From each fabric, cut 2 — 2½" strip across the length.
From each fabric, cut 5 — 2½" squares.

### REDS

From each fabric, cut 3 — 2½" strips across the length.

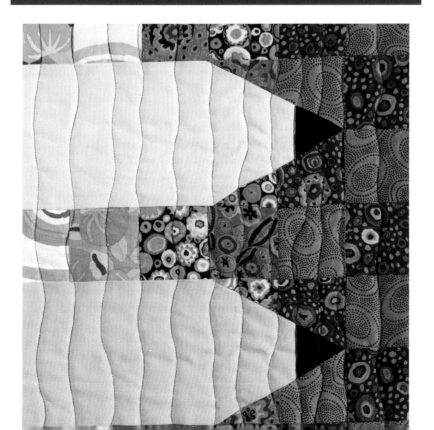

## PIECING

### BACKGROUND

Sew together a color pair of strips (red to red, orange to orange, and so on). Press the seam to the darker strip.

Crosscut the strips into 2½" squares to yield:
- 8 sets of orange
- 8 sets of yellow
- 8 sets of green
- 8 sets of blue
- 8 sets of indigo
- 13 sets of violet
- 18 sets of red

Make the first and third rows by sewing 1 pair of each color end to end, with the lighter square of each pair on the left.

Make the second and fourth rows by sewing 1 pair of each color end to end, with the darker square of each pair on the left.

For the top and bottom rows, start by sewing 2 rectangle pairs of each color into a single color four-patch. Sew the four-patches together with 1 of the light squares of each four-patch in the upper left corner.

## PENCILS

From the leftover red rectangles, piece to make 5 more red four-patches.

5 x

Using the indigo and violet squares, make pairs of the lighter indigo with the darker violet and the darker indigo with the lighter violet. Sew each pair together. Press toward the darker fabric. This yields 10 sets of 2 squares.

Using the indigo and violet squares, make pairs — sew together. Press toward the darker fabric. This yields 5 sets of 2 squares.

5 x

Cut each indigo/violet pair at an angle as shown:

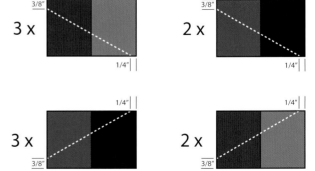

Group the pairs into 5 sets. Each pair should have opposite angles and opposite colors.

Attach each 2" black square to each large gray rectangle by centering the square on 1 end of the rectangle:

Using the triangle pairs from the previous step, match them up with the corresponding pencil. Working from the top, the set of 3 pairs go with the first, third, and fifth pencils. The set of 2 pairs go with the second and fourth pencils. Starting with the first pencil, lay the top triangle on the end of the pencil, matching the seams — all pieces are right side up. Using chalk, mark the line where the angled edge of the triangle meets the pencil (yellow line below). Cut the seam allowance on the pencil ½" from this line (red line below). Attach the triangle. Press. Repeat with the other side of the pencil point as shown:

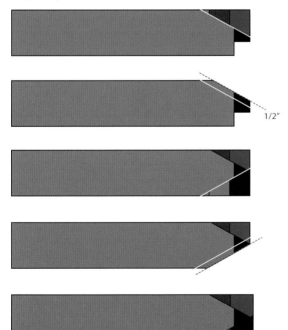

1/2"

Continue this with all 5 pencils.

## ASSEMBLY

Lay out the entire quilt:

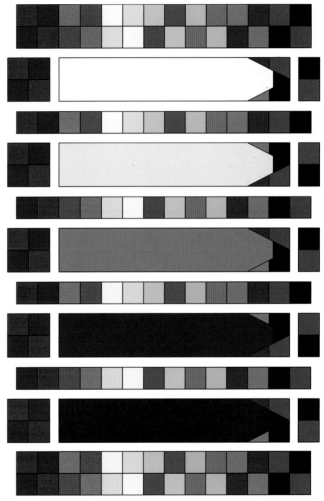

Stitch the red four-patch and the violet two-patch to either end of each pencil making sure the dark and light of each color alternate (refer to the quilt photo, page 40). Press.

Stitch the rows together. Press.

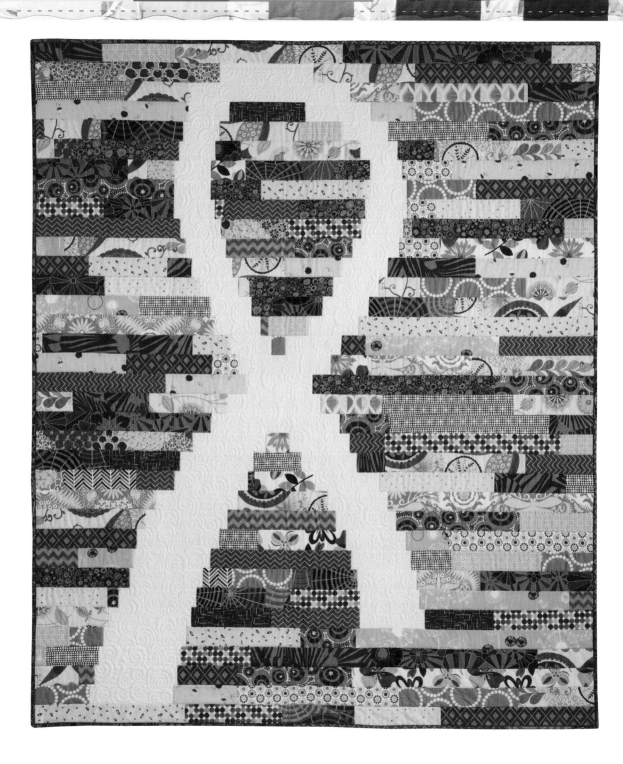

It is easy to turn a non-linear design element into something that is linear and simple to piece. In *Aware*, I just drew an awareness ribbon on a piece of graph paper. Then I went row-by-row and drew a seam line where the outline of the ribbon crossed the grid. Be smart about this and keep in mind that you'll have to cut it out. So, stick with measurements of halves and quarters when dividing a grid so that there aren't any $\frac{7}{8}$" or $\frac{1}{16}$" increments to deal with in the end.

While this version of *Aware* denotes breast cancer awareness, the colors can be changed to reflect the cause of your choice.

### *Aware* Fabric Details

The solid is Kona snow. I wanted this quilt to represent breast cancer awareness, so I wanted a lot of different pink fabrics. I pulled all the pinks from my stash — which was pretty lacking. I filled in with fabrics from my local quilt shops — getting a quarter yard of just about every modern pink fabric I could find. I made the binding from the scraps and used a solid pink flange to separate the binding from the quilt — which was a little chaotic side-by-side.

## FABRIC REQUIREMENTS

1 yard cream
18 — ¼ yard cuts of various pink prints
(4½ yards total)

## CUTTING

### CREAM

Cut 11 — 2½" wide strips across the width of fabric.

Crosscut according to this table:

| Quantity | Length |
|---|---|
| 1 | 4 |
| 7 | 4½ |
| 9 | 5 |
| 6 | 5½ |
| 1 | 6 |
| 2 | 6½ |
| 7 | 7 |
| 4 | 7½ |
| 4 | 8½ |
| 2 | 9 |
| 8 | 9½ |
| 3 | 10½ |
| 1 | 14½ |
| 1 | 17½ |

## PINKS

To prepare the pieced pink strips, cut 52 — 2½" strips x wof.

Crosscut the shorter pieces (up to about 17"). Cut the remaining strips into smaller pieces (in varying lengths less than 15") and piece together, then finish cutting the longer pieces.

| Quantity | Length | Quantity | Length | Quantity | Length |
|---|---|---|---|---|---|
| 1 | 2 | 1 | 12½ | 5 | 21½ |
| 1 | 3 | 2 | 13½ | 4 | 22½ |
| 2 | 5½ | 2 | 14 | 3 | 23½ |
| 1 | 6½ | 6 | 15½ | 2 | 24½ |
| 1 | 7 | 3 | 16 | 2 | 25½ |
| 2 | 7½ | 4 | 16½ | 2 | 26½ |
| 2 | 8 | 2 | 17 | 2 | 27½ |
| 2 | 8½ | 5 | 17½ | 1 | 28½ |
| 1 | 9½ | 1 | 18 | 1 | 29½ |
| 1 | 10 | 3 | 18½ | 2 | 30½ |
| 2 | 10½ | 1 | 19 | 1 | 44 |
| 1 | 11 | 3 | 19½ | 1 | 44½ |
| 1 | 11½ | 2 | 20 | 1 | 45 |
| 2 | 12 | 4 | 20½ | 1 | 45½ |
|  |  | 2 | 21 | 2 | 60½ |

Lay out the strips according to the diagram.

Piece the rows together. Press all seams to 1 side. Where the seams match up, press the seams so they oppose each other.

## ASSEMBLY

Sew the rows together.

| | | | | | |
|---|---|---|---|---|---|
| 60 ½" | | | | | |
| 20 ½" | 10 ½" | | | 30 ½" | |
| 17 ½" | 17 ½" | | | 26 ½" | |
| 17" | 5" | 8 ½" | 7 ½" | 24 ½" | |
| 16 ½" | 4 ½" | 13 ½" | 5 ½" | 22 ½" | |
| 16" | 4 ½" | 16" | 4 ½" | 21 ½" | |
| 15 ½" | 4 ½" | 17 ½" | 4" | 21" | |
| 15 ½" | 4 ½" | 17 ½" | 4 ½" | 20 ½" | |
| 15 ½" | 5" | 16 ½" | 5" | 20 ½" | |
| 16" | 5" | 15 ½" | 5" | 21" | |
| 16 ½" | 5" | 14" | 5 ½" | 21 ½" | |
| 17 ½" | 5" | 12" | 5 ½" | 22 ½" | |
| 18 ½" | 4 ½" | 10 ½" | 5 ½" | 23 ½" | |
| 19 ½" | 5" | 8" | 5 ½" | 24 ½" | |
| 20" | 5 ½" | 5 ½" | 6" | 25 ½" | |
| 21 ½" | 5" | 2" | 6 ½" | 27 ½" | |
| 22 ½" | 10 ½" | | | 28 ½" | |
| 23 ½" | 7 ½" | | | 30 ½" | |
| 21 ½" | 10 ½" | | | 29 ½" | |
| 19 ½" | 14 ½" | | | 27 ½" | |
| 17 ½" | 8 ½" | 3" | 7" | 26 ½" | |
| 16 ½" | 8 ½" | 5 ½" | 6 ½" | 25 ½" | |
| 15 ½" | 8 ½" | 7 ½" | 7 ½" | 23 ½" | |
| 13 ½" | 9 ½" | 10" | 7" | 22 ½" | |
| 12 ½" | 9 ½" | 12" | 7" | 21 ½" | |
| 11 ½" | 9 ½" | 14" | 7" | 20 ½" | |
| 11" | 9" | 15 ½" | 7" | 20" | |
| 10 ½" | 8 ½" | 17" | 7" | 19 ½" | |
| 9 ½" | 9" | 18" | 7" | 19" | |
| 8 ½" | 9 ½" | 18 ½" | 7 ½" | 18 ½" | |
| 8" | 9 ½" | 44" | | | |
| 7 ½" | 9 ½" | 44 ½" | | | |
| 7" | 9 ½" | 45" | | | |
| 6 ½" | 9 ½" | 45 ½" | | | |
| 60 ½" | | | | | |

# INTERRUPTION

An interrupted design carries the negative space into the positive design to create a secondary image. These designs have broken lines and your brain will naturally complete the lines — which is what makes these quilts exciting.

The key to designing an interruption is to have a simple quilt design for the base of the quilt. All of the quilts in this chapter start with a very linear-based design. The key in designing is juxtaposition. Generally speaking, mixing a linear-based quilt with curved interruptions will highlight the secondary design. In comparing the quilts in this chapter, you can see that the curved interruptions in *String of Pearls* (page 50) and *Hoops and Stix* (page 60) are more overt than the linear interruptions of *Seventh Inning* (page 54).

In *String of Pearls*, the white negative space bleeds into the circles that overlay the positive design. In *Hoops and Stix*, the negative space bleeds through the ovals that cross over the sticks. In *Seventh Inning*, the sashing serves as the negative space and bleeds into the blocks to create a very subtle baseball diamond.

This quilt was inspired by a couple of charm packs. Since I don't like the pinked edges on precuts, I added longer lengths of fabric from the same line. That way, I could line everything up with the straight-cut edges. The base is comprised of simply pieced, colorful lines of varying length and position. The background fabric is cut at varying widths to keep it interesting. Then I overlaid a design comprised of circles set within a circle. I like things with mathematical relevance, so I tend to look for mathematical patterns when I design — so there is a method behind the placement of the circles. I like the way your eye has to complete the lines of the circles as they pass through the negative space.

### *String of Pearls* Fabric Details

The solid is Kona white. The print is Lizzy House's Pearl Bracelets from the Andover fabrics booth at QuiltCon 2013. With a little swapping, I ended up with two charm packs — what are friends for! There wasn't quite enough to make the quilt, so I bought five more pieces to fill in.

## FABRIC REQUIREMENTS

Two charm packs (a total of 50 charm 5" squares)
Fat quarter each of 5 different prints
3 yards white background

## SUPPLIES

Compass (or other way of making circles size 1½" to 8½" finished)
Tape measure
Straight pins

## CUTTING

### PRINT

Cut the charm packs in half down the center to make 100 — 2½" x 5" rectangles.
Cut 25 — 2½" strips from fat quarters.

### BACKGROUND

Cut 9 — 2½" x wof strips to finish print strips.
From the remaining length of fabric, cut strips the following widths about 80" long:

- 5 — 2" strips
- 6 — 2½" strips
- 4 — 3" strips
- 2 — 3½" strips

This will use all 44" of the width. If your fabric is less than that, you can either cut a few of the strips thinner or cut extra from the original width of fabric and piece 2 together to get an equivalent length.

## PIECING

Piece the 2½" print strips, varying lengths and colors, in 16 columns up to 70" long. Press. Using the 2½" x wof background strips, add pieces of varying lengths to the ends of each column to make each approximately 80" long. Press. Refer to the photo of the quilt on page 50 for placement.

Lay out the pieced columns alternating with the long background strips. Make sure to spread out the different widths of the background strips throughout the entire top. Piece together and press to the dark.

Prepare 9 circles for appliqué in your favorite method. The finished size of each are: 1½", 2", 2½", 3½", 4½", 5½", 6½", 7½", 8½". *(Turned-edge applique will need a seam allowance, fusible won't.)*

## ASSEMBLY

Mark a center point 28" from the right hand edge and 35" from the bottom. Place the end of a measuring tape at this point. This is easiest to do on a pin-able surface. Place 2 straight pins through the hole at the end of the tape measure at opposing angles to hold the tape securely. Draw a circle — or mark it with pins — at the end of the 16" measure. The circles are placed within a large circle with a radius of 16" and the distance between the circles varies: the smaller the circles, the smaller the distance. Starting with ¾" between the smallest 2 circles, increase the distance by ¼" as the circles get larger: ¾", 1", 1¼", 1½", 1¾", 2", 2¼", 2½". Appliqué the circles in place.

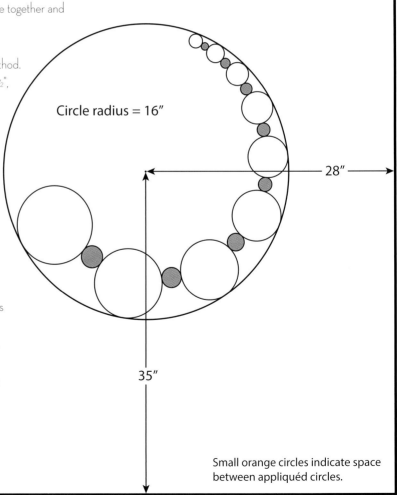

Circle radius = 16"

28"

35"

Small orange circles indicate space between appliquéd circles.

## QUILTING

Ida Houston of Cowtown Quilts quilted *String of Pearls* to complement the quilt without detracting from it. Knowing the quilt name, Ida tried to work strings of pearls throughout the quilt. She also wanted to emphasize the different sized circles by repeating them in the quilting. Knowing that if not quilted, the circles would poof up a lot, she stitched different quilting designs to fill the circles. Through these designs, Ida sought the effect of being near the ocean, where pearls are found. The background filler accents the strips.

Ida is known for sneaking little surprises into her customers' quilts. These surprises are intended to make her customers smile and give a personal touch for each quiltmaker, so that he or she will have an heirloom like no other. For more about Ida, see; www.cowtownquilts.wordpress.com.

As if it's not hard enough to find a quilt design that a boy would love, try finding a design that they will continue to love as they get older. That's what I had in mind when I designed this baseball-themed quilt. While it doesn't scream baseball, the idea is definitely there. This is another quilt that requires some examination to see the design — I love quilt designs that are not "in your face." At its foundation, this quilt is simply made of 25 blocks each made of five rectangles with a simple sashing. The sashing serves as the negative space. The excitement comes when the negative space bleeds into the primary design to create the image of a baseball diamond.

## *Seventh Inning* Fabric Details

The light solid is Kona meringue. The greens were all pulled from my stash — some are Kona, Moda Crossweaves, Michael Miller's Mirror Ball Dot, whatever green-ish solid-ish fabrics I could find. The binding is from a black and green stripy fabric that has been in my stash for more than 15 years.

## FABRIC REQUIREMENTS

A total of 2¾ yards assorted greens (10 or more)
2 yards light yellow/cream

## CUTTING

### YELLOW

Cut 4 strips 2½" x 58½" across the length of the fabric (the remaining width of fabric is approximately 30").
Cut 2 strips 10½" across the remaining width of fabric:
  • Crosscut 20 — 2½" x 10½" rectangles.
  • Crosscut 6 — 1½" x 10½".
Cut an 8½" strip across the remaining width of fabric:
  • Crosscut 1 — 3½" x 8½" rectangle.
  • Crosscut 1 — 1½" x 8½" rectangle.
  • Crosscut 1 — 1½" x 7½" rectangle.
  • Crosscut 2 — 1½" x 2½" rectangles.
  • Cut 3 — 6½" squares.
From remaining fabric, cut a 7⅞" square; cut across the diagonal to get a half-square-triangle (only 1 triangle is needed).

## GREEN

Cut 6 — 10½" strips:

- Crosscut 88 — 2½" x 10½".
- Crosscut 3 — 1½" x 10½".

Cut an 8⅞" square, then cut diagonally to get 2 half-square triangles.

Cut a 5⅜" square, then cut diagonally to get 2 half-square triangles.

Cut 1 — 7½" strip:

- Crosscut 16 — 2½" x 7½".

Cut a 7⅞" strip:

- Crosscut 1 — 7⅞" square, then cut diagonally to get a half-square triangle.

From the remaining half-square triangle, cut a 4¼" quarter-square triangle.

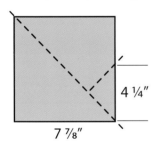

4 ¼"

7 ⅞"

From the remaining strip, cut 3 — 2½" x wof strips:

- Crosscut 37 — 2½" x 2½".
- Crosscut 1 — 1½" x 2½".

## PIECING

All blocks measure 10½" square unfinished.

### MAKE 14 BLOCK A, USING:

5 — 2½" x 10½"

### MAKE 1 BLOCK B:

Piece 3 — 2½" x 2½" — 2 sets; attach to each side of the square. Press to the square.

Piece 2½" x 2½" + 1½" x 2½" + 2½" x 7½". Press to the green.

Attach the top and bottom strips to the center.

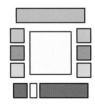

### 1 BLOCK C:

Piece 3 — 2½" x 2½" — 2 sets; attach to each side of the square. Press to the square.

Attach the top and bottom strips to the center.

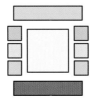

## 1 BLOCK D:

Piece 3 — 2½" x 2½" — 1 set.

Piece 2 — 2½" x 2½" + yellow 1½" x 2½" + green 1½" x 2½".

Attach to each side of the square. Press toward the square.

Attach the top and bottom strips to the center.

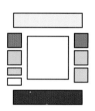 

## 1 BLOCK E:

Stitch a small green quarter-square triangle to each end of the yellow triangle. Press and trim.

Attach a 7⅞" green half-square triangle.

Attach a shorter yellow strip to 1 side. Attach the longer one to the adjacent side.

Piece 4 — 2½" x 2½" — 1 set. Attach to the side.

Add the 2½" x 10½" strip.

 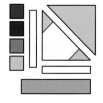 

## 3 BLOCK F:

Piece 3 — 2½" x 10½" + green 1½" x 10½" + yellow 1½" x 10½" + green 2½" x 10½".

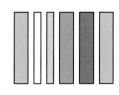 

## 3 BLOCK G:

Piece 5 — 2½" x 7½".

Piece 5 — 2½" x 2½".

Attach with the yellow strip in between.

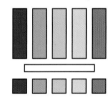 

## 1 BLOCK H:

Center a 8⅞" half-square triangle on a yellow 3½" x 8½" rectangle and stitch. Press. Repeat on the other side. Trim the green triangles to be even with yellow.

Center 5⅜" half-square triangles on each side and stitch. Press.

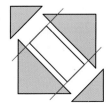

## ASSEMBLY

Refer to the diagram on the next page. Attach 10½" sashing between the blocks to make 5 rows.

Using chalk, mark the long sashing strips to indicate where to match seams: 10¼" from 1 end, 2", 10", 2", 10", 2", 10", 2". Attach, matching the marks on the sashing with the corresponding block seams. Stitch together.

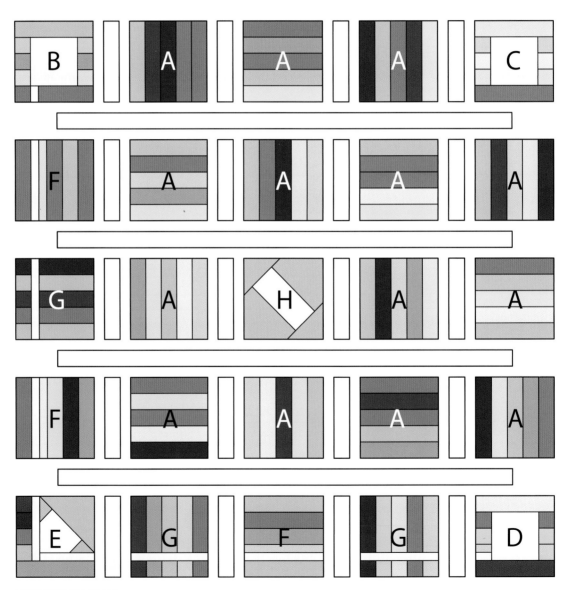

ASSEMBLY DIAGRAM

The foundation of this quilt is pretty straightforward: it is a large background with straight lines running through it at slight angles. Simple. Then the ovals are added. They are effectively broken when they cross into the background — your brain reconnects the ovals.

Upon initial inspection, this quilt may seem a little daunting to make. All of those pieces of the ovals have to line up. The key is appliqué and bias tape. There are many options for the appliqué: you can hand stitch, machine stitch, or glue baste (then stitch down the appliqué when the top is quilted).

### *Hoops and Stix* Fabric Details

All of the fabrics are Kona cottons. I started building the 'stix' with fabrics that are in the same family as the background (Kona cinnamon) to add some depth to the design. I ended with contrasting accents in green and blue.

# Hoops and Stix

## FABRIC REQUIREMENTS

5½ yards rust background
½ yard light blue
¼ yard light green
¼ yard light yellow
½ yard orange-yellow
½ yard orange
½ yard caramel

## SUPPLIES

Chalk, long acrylic ruler (6" x 24"), starch

## CUTTING

### BACKGROUND

Cut 2 — 2¼ yard lengths from the rust background.
From the remaining yardage, cut 2¼" bias strips (at 45°):
- 2 strips around 48"
- 2 strips around 36"
- 2 strips around 30"

Use the rest of the fabric for binding.

### LIGHT GREEN, LIGHT YELLOW, ORANGE

Cut 4 strips from each color 2" x wof

### LIGHT BLUE, ORANGE-YELLOW

Cut 6 strips from each color 2" x wof

### CARAMEL

Cut 8 strips 2" x wof

## PIECING

Taking 2 strips of 1 color, attach by sewing across the 2" seam to make 1 long strip. Press the seams to one side. Continue until all of the strips have been paired up. This will yield long strips: 2 light green, 2 light yellow, 2 orange, 3 light blue, 3 orange-yellow, 4 caramel.

Lay the 2 background pieces side-by-side, overlapping them by a few inches. Make a chalk mark at the top of each piece to help orient the fabric. Mark a line with chalk at a slight angle down the overlap. Cut both layers along the line. Insert 1 caramel strip, pressing as you go. In general, seams are pressed to the background, unless needed to reduce bulk.

Lay the quilt completely flat. Mark a line with chalk in the left area, then cut. (Warning: if you cut without marking, the line will tend to shift as you are cutting.) Insert another strip of caramel. Press.

Continue inserting the strips: 1 at a time, distributing the colors across the quilt. Insert the strips in this order: caramel, light yellow, yellow-orange, orange, green, and blue. When inserting a strip, if it crosses another strip cut out an extra 1" from the seam allowance. This will help to keep the lines flowing across the strips in a straight line without having to shift the background. This is especially important if a strip crosses more than 1 strip.

## BIAS TAPE

To make the bias tape, mark the bias strips along the length of each strip at 1½" and ¾" using chalk. Lightly spray with starch. Press each side, folding the raw edge to the closest mark.

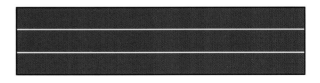

Fold

Fold

## ASSEMBLY

Lay the quilt top flat. Each piece of bias will make one-half of an oval. Lay out the ovals in the general shape you want. With a pin-able pressing mat underneath, lightly spray the bias with starch. Press and pin the strip to make the final shape. Lay out the ovals so the ends meet with a background seam or can be slipped under another piece of bias tape. When the ovals are final, use a seam ripper to open the adjacent seam allowance and pull the tail through. Restitch the seams. Press.

Appliqué the bias tape down either by hand or machine.

## HOW TO MAKE FABRIC STRIPS ALIGN

When you insert a fabric strip into the background, you add space/width. If the strip is ½" finished, everything works (because it takes up the space — ¼" seam allowance on each side). If it's larger than that, the other strips won't flow correctly.

The solution: remove fabric from the background. The amount you need to remove is: the finished width of the strip minus ½" (because of the space made by the seam allowances of the background fabric).

If the finished width is 1½", remove an extra 1" from the seam allowance.

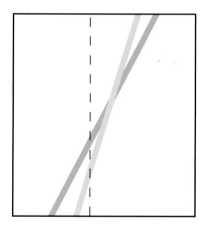

DASHED LINE = CUTTING LINE.

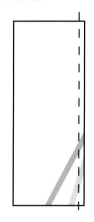 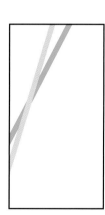

TO FIX — REMOVE FINISHED WIDTH OF THE STRIP MINUS ½" (CUT AT DASHED LINE).

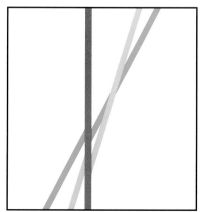

ADDING STRIP LARGER THAN ½" FINISHED = OTHER STRIPS DO NOT ALIGN.

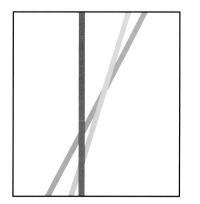

STRIPS ALIGN.

# NEGATIVE FORM

Negative Form design starts with a bold, graphic shape. The shape becomes the negative space of the quilt design and piecing is planned around the shape. In *Raindrop* (page 64), the shape is a large raindrop set off to one side. The remaining space is filled with simple rows of random piecing. In *Silk Bricks* (page 70), the shape is an arc. Simple bricks made of concentric rectangles fill in the surrounding space. *Fibonacci Spiral* (page 74) is based on a graphic shape by the same name. The line of the graph is formed by the piecing.

The piecing in this quilt is simple rows. Prints in a wide array of colors evoke the feeling of a rainy day. These prints are intermingled with the solid used in the negative space to give the pieced area some breathing room. The pieced area is approximately one-third solid and two-thirds prints. For a more colorful quilt, increase the number of strips cut from the prints and decrease the number of solid strips.

## *Raindrop* Fabric Details

The solid is Kona ash. I pulled the prints from my stash, looking for any colors that I perceived as 'rainy' — blues, purples, pinks. I filled in with prints from my local quilt shop, buying a quarter yard at a time.

## FABRIC REQUIREMENTS

3 yards light gray
Total of 2 yards print scraps

## SUPPLIES

Chalk
Flexible curve or tracing paper

## CUTTING

### LIGHT GRAY

Reserve a 2 yard piece for the raindrop.
Cut 24 strips 1½" x wof, crosscut into
   random lengths approximately 6" to 36".

### PRINTS

Cut 1½" wide print scraps into varying
   lengths (approximately 6" to 24").
   You need about 1,800" (50 yards) in
   total length.

## PIECING

Randomly piece together the prints and the solid strips into 1 long continuous length. As you cut the pieces, alternate between the ends so that you don't get the same fabrics next to each other. Cut the pieces according to the table. As you cut, either label the lengths or keep them in order to aid in the piecing process.

Piece all of the rows on the left side of the quilt. Start stitching each seam from the left edge of the quilt; the right side will be uneven. As you go, press each seam toward the bottom of the quilt.

| Left-hand side | | | Right-hand side | |
|---|---|---|---|---|
| 7 — 42½" | 34" | 25" | 7 — 18½" | 9" |
| 2 — 42" | 33½" | 6 — 24½" | 18" | 8" |
| 2 — 41½" | 33" | 4 — 25" | 2 — 17½" | 7½" |
| 41" | 32" | 25½" | 2 — 17" | 7" |
| 40½" | 31½" | 2 — 26" | 16½" | 6½" |
| 2 — 40" | 31" | 26½" | 16" | 6" |
| 39½" | 30½" | 27" | 2 — 15½" | 5½" |
| 39" | 30" | 27½" | 2 — 14½" | 5" |
| 38½" | 29½" | 28" | 14" | 4½" |
| 38" | 29" | 29" | 13½" | 4" |
| 37½" | 28½" | 29½" | 13" | 3½" |
| 37" | 28" | 31" | 12" | 3" |
| 36½" | 27" | 32½" | 11½" | 2½" |
| 36" | 26½" | 34" | 11" | 2" |
| 35½" | 26" | 35½" | 10" | 2 — 1½" |
| 35" | 25½" | 37½" | 9½" | 1" |
| | | 38½" | | |

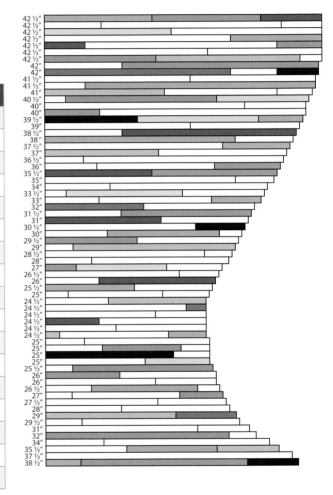

Continue piecing the rows of the right side. Start each seam from the right edge of the quilt; the left side will be uneven. Press each seam as you go, pressing toward the top.

## ASSEMBLY

Lay out the left side. With a rotary cutter, trim to create a curve, making a raindrop shape using the uneven ends as a guide (think dot-to-dot!). Repeat with the right side.

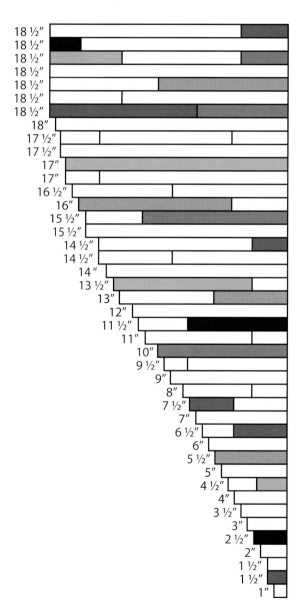

18 ½"
18 ½"
18 ½"
18 ½"
18 ½"
18 ½"
18 ½"
18"
17 ½"
17 ½"
17"
17"
16 ½"
16"
15 ½"
15 ½"
14 ½"
14 ½"
14"
13 ½"
13"
12"
11 ½"
11"
10"
9 ½"
9"
8"
7 ½"
7"
6 ½"
6"
5 ½"
5"
4 ½"
4"
3 ½"
3"
2 ½"
2"
1 ½"
1 ½"
1"

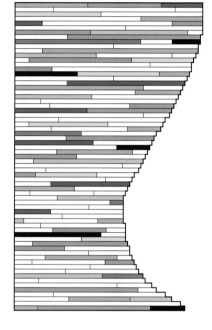

BEFORE TRIMMING.

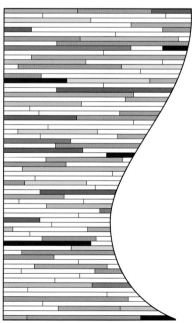

AFTER TRIMMING —
SMOOTH CURVE.

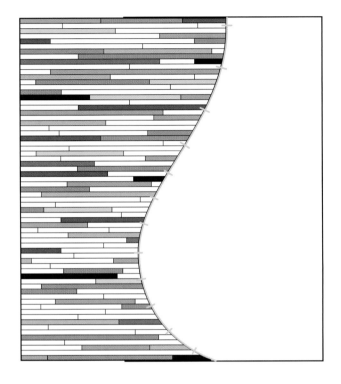

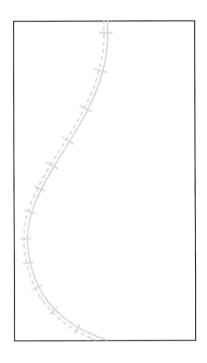

Lay out the reserved light gray. Place the left side of the quilt on top, ensuring there is a generous amount of overlap (at least ½"). Transfer the curve line onto the light gray with chalk. Using the chalk, mark about 12 registration lines by drawing across both fabrics perpendicular to the curve (shown in green in the diagram above). Remove the left side. Mark another curve ½" from the curve (into what will be the seam allowance). Extend the registration lines into the seam allowance. Cut on the last curve drawn. Stitch the pieces together, matching the registration points.

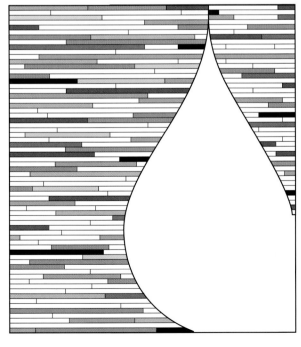

Repeat with the right side, lining up the top 4 rows with a ½" overlap. To stitch, match up the first 4 rows, then match the registration marks. Press.

After the quilting is complete, trim the bottom right corner. Using a flexible curve, form it to the left side of the curve. Flip it over and use it to mark the curve on the right side. After the entire curve is marked, trim. Note: tracing paper can be used if a flexible curve isn't available.

## FINISHING

To bind the quilt, make sure the binding that butts up against the curve is cut on the bias.

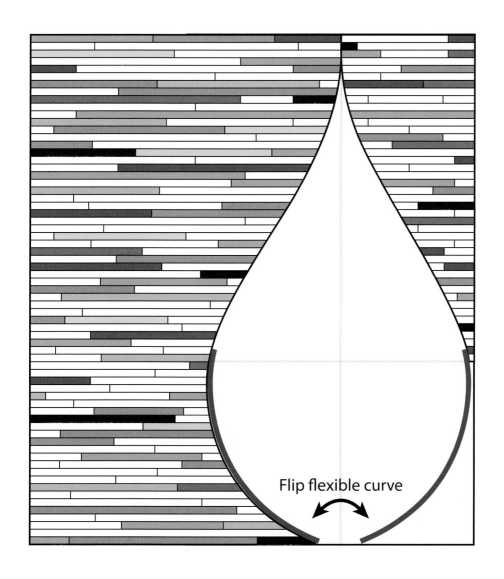

Flip flexible curve

# Silk Bricks

SIZE: 30" X 40"

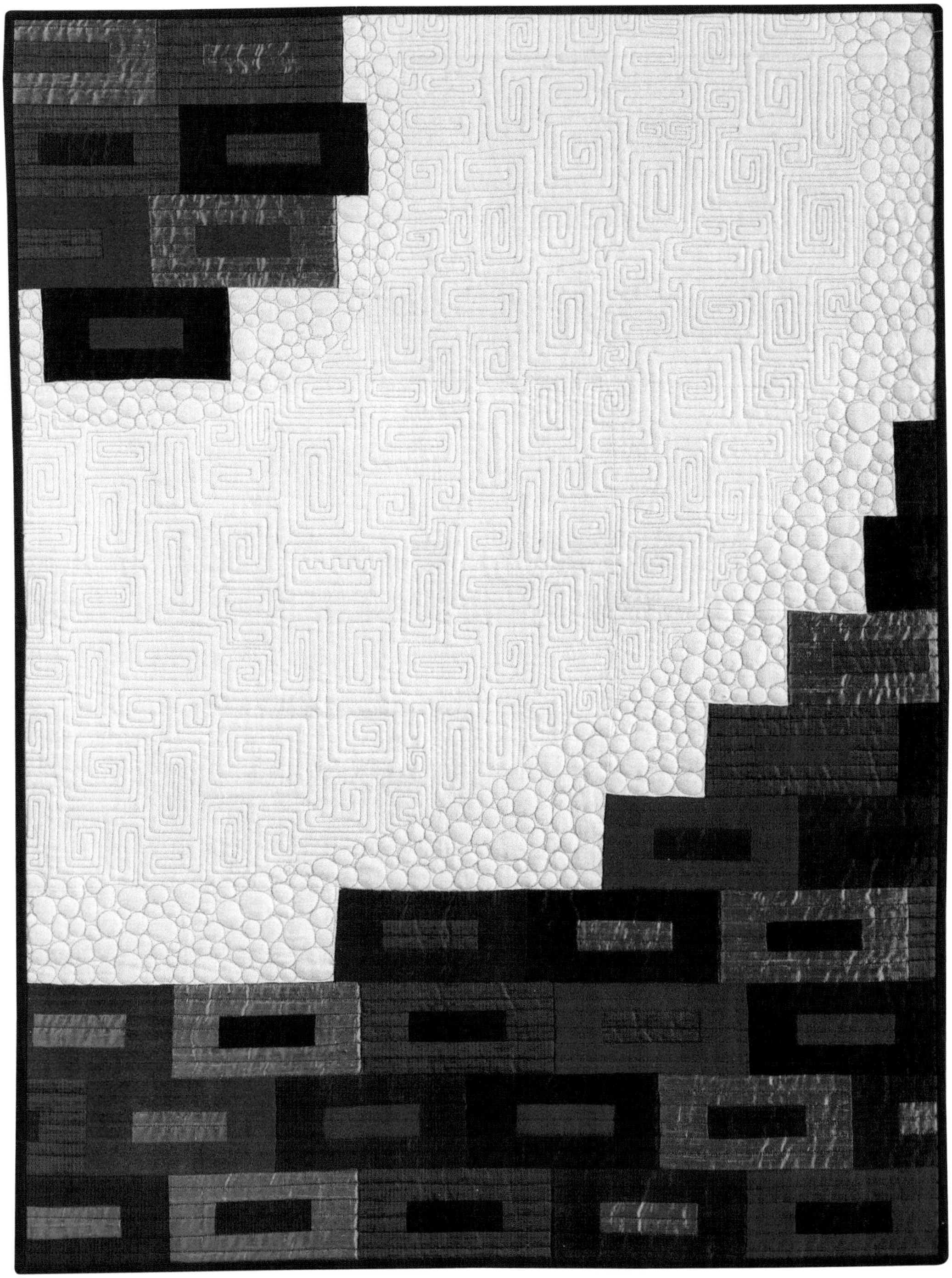

*Silk Bricks* was designed around an arc shape. It was drafted on graph paper. First, I drew two concentric arcs. This shape defines the negative space. The bricks were drafted around the arcs to fill in the positive space. The bricks are all the same size and alternately stacked. The quilting further emphasizes the arc.

## *Silk Bricks* Fabric Details

The solid is natural linen. I prewashed the linen to get it as stable as possible, then starched it. It still moved around a lot. If you are not an experienced quilter, I would recommend against using natural linen. There are a lot of cotton fabrics made to look like linen which would be a lot easier to use. The colors are all silk dupioni that I bought at QuiltCon 2013. I didn't bother to stabilize the silk — it's easy to piece if everything is cut on the straight of grain. If you go with silk, here are three pieces of advice: it's probably going to bleed; keep a lint roller handy because it's messy; and keep hand lotion nearby! If you don't want to use silks, I think Oakshott cottons would be a great substitute.

## FABRIC REQUIREMENTS

¾ yard neutral linen (to allow for shrinkage)
5 fat quarters of silk dupioni

## CUTTING

### LINEN

Cut 1 — 3½" strip, then crosscut:
11½", 8½", 6", 5", 3½", 1½", 1½", 1¼"

From the remaining fabric, cut the following rectangles:
- 16½" x 19½"
- 18½" x 12½"
- 9½" x 4½"
- 2½" x 1½"

### SILK DUPIONI

From the silks, cut:
31 — 1½" x 3½"
31 sets (all 4 pieces from the same fabric):
- 2 — 1½" x 2"
- 2 — 1½" x 6½"

## PIECING

Start piecing the silk bricks. Pair up each 4 piece set with 1 of the 1½" x 3½" rectangles of a different color. Piece the rectangles according to the diagram:

Cut 3 of the completed bricks:

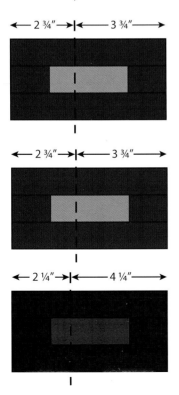

Piece the quilt according to the diagram on the next page.

Trim the sides:

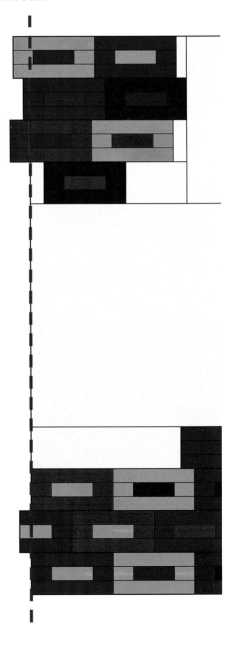

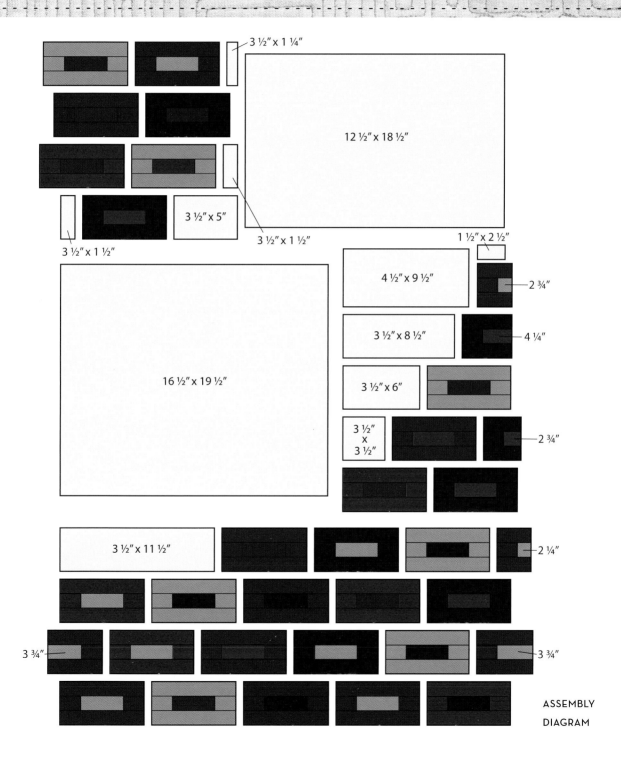

3 ½" x 1 ¼"

3 ½" x 5"

3 ½" x 1 ½"

3 ½" x 1 ½"

12 ½" x 18 ½"

1 ½" x 2 ½"

4 ½" x 9 ½"

2 ¾"

3 ½" x 8 ½"

4 ¼"

3 ½" x 6"

16 ½" x 19 ½"

3 ½"
x
3 ½"

2 ¾"

3 ½" x 11 ½"

2 ¼"

3 ¾"

3 ¾"

ASSEMBLY
DIAGRAM

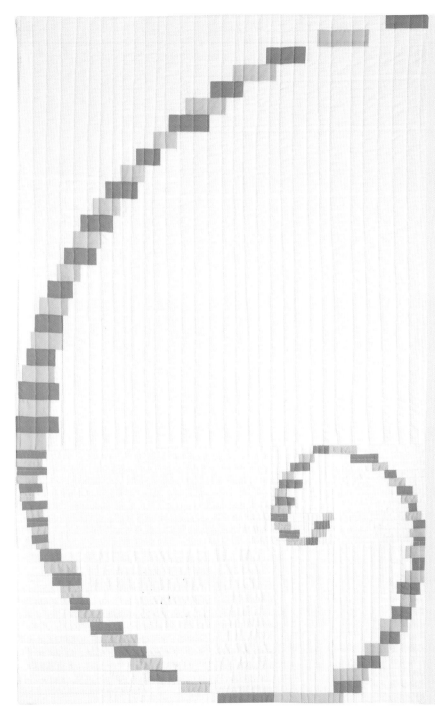

*Fibonacci Spiral* was designed around a line. The concept is based on the Fibonacci Series that we all know and love from middle school math class! If you are not familiar with the spiral, a quick search on the internet can answer all of your questions.

To interpret this line into a quilt, I drew the shape on a sheet of graph paper. I went row by row and drew a seam line where the graph crossed the row — with standard increments (not smaller than ¼") in mind. From there, I wanted the colors to fall to the inside of the spiral, so I marked off the colored pieces at random lengths into the spiral shape. Keep in mind that you don't want to make pieces any more accurate than you are willing to cut. I tried to keep my marks at ¼", or better yet, ½" intervals.

### *Fibonacci Spiral* Fabric Details

This quilt is made of Kona cottons. The colors are from my "go-to" palette — turquoise and chartreuse.

# FABRIC REQUIREMENTS

⅛ yard green

⅛ yard blue

1¼ yards white for background

# CUTTING

## GREEN

Cut 1 — 1" strip.

Crosscut:

- 3 — 1¼"
- 7 — 1½"
- 3 — 1¾"
- 1 — 2¼"

Cut 1 — 1¼" strip

Crosscut:

- 1 — 1¼"
- 1 — 1½"
- 3 — 1¾"
- 1 — 1⅞"
- 3 — 2"
- 3 — 2¼"
- 2 — 2½"
- 2 — 2¾"
- 1 — 4½"

Cut 1 — 1½" strip.

Crosscut:

- 3 — 2"
- 3 — 2¼"
- 4 — 2½"
- 2 — 3"
- 1 — 3¾"

## BLUE

Cut 1 — 1" strip.

Crosscut:

- 1 — 1"
- 3 — 1¼"
- 4 — 1½"
- 4 — 1¾"
- 1 — 2"
- 1 — 2¼"

Cut 1 — 1¼" strip.

Crosscut:

- 1 — 1⅜"
- 3 — 1½"
- 2 — 1¾"
- 4 — 2"
- 3 — 2¼"
- 3 — 2½"
- 1 — 3½"

Cut 1 — 1½" strip.

Crosscut:

- 2 — 2"
- 3 — 2¼"
- 3 — 2½"
- 3 — 3"
- 1 — 3⅛"
- 1 — 3½"

## WHITE BACKGROUND

Cut 2 — 1" strips.

Crosscut:

- 6 — ¾"
- 6 — 1"
- 7 — 1¼"
- 7 — 1½"

- 1 — 1¾"
- 2 — 2"
- 1 — 2¼"
- 1 — 2½"
- 1 — 2¾"
- 2 — 3"
- 4 — 3¼"
- 1 — 3½"
- 1 — 4¾"

Cut 3 — 1¼" strips.

Crosscut:

- 4 — ¾"
- 2 — ⅞"
- 5 — 1"
- 6 — 1¼"
- 3 — 1½"
- 4 — 1¾"
- 3 — 2"
- 3 — 2¼"
- 4 — 2½"
- 1 — 2¾"
- 2 — 3"
- 1 — 3¼"
- 2 — 3½"
- 1 — 4¼"
- 1 — 4½"
- 2 — 4¾"
- 1 — 5"
- 1 — 7"

Cut 3 — 1½" strips.

Crosscut:

- 4 — ¾"
- 1 — ⅝"
- 5 — 1"
- 2 — 1¼"

- 6 — 1½"
- 2 — 1¾"
- 3 — 2"
- 1 — 2¼"
- 5 — 2½"
- 4 — 3"
- 3 — 3½"
- 2 — 3¾"
- 1 — 4½"
- 1 — 8"

Cut the remaining pieces:

- 1 — 2" x 4½"
- 1 — 2½" x 8½"
- 2 — 2¾" x 3½"
- 1 — 2¾" x 5½"
- 1 — 3½" x 3½"
- 2 — 3½" x 5½"
- 1 — 3½" x 8½"
- 1 — 3½" x 12½"
- 1 — 4½" x 6½"
- 1 — 4½" x 7"
- 1 — 4½" x 16½"
- 1 — 5" x 5¾"
- 1 — 6½" x 14½"
- 1 — 7" x 10½"
- 1 — 7½" x 20"
- 1 — 8½" x 9½"
- 1 — 8½" x 23½"

## PIECING

Piece the rows according to the diagram. Red circles indicate partial seams — leave at least 2" unstitched.

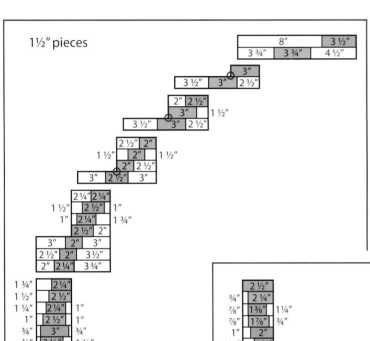

1½" pieces

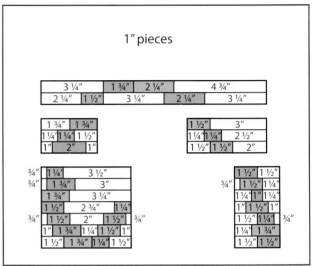

1" pieces

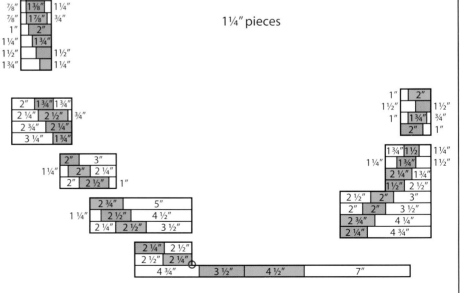

1¼" pieces

**CONTINUE TO ADD THE BACKGROUND PIECES.**

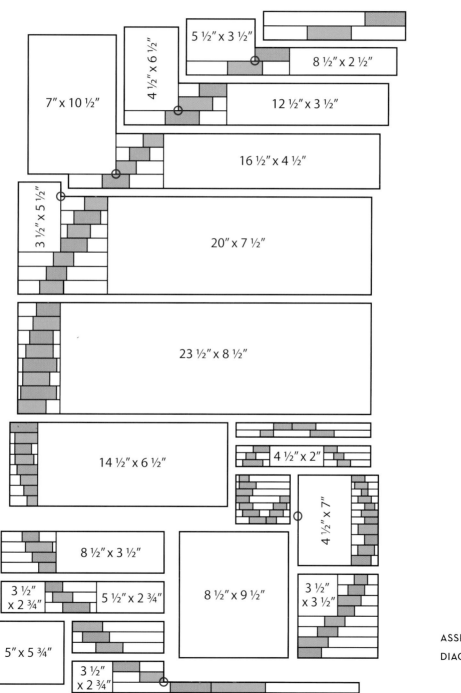

ASSEMBLY

DIAGRAM

# GHOSTING

Ghosting occurs when the positive image is referenced in the negative space with a "shadow" of the block that generally blends with the background. The key to getting a good ghost is contrast. The pieces that you want to appear in the foreground should be high contrast — larger, brighter prints, preferably in pure hues (not shades, tones, or tints). As you move away from the foreground, the fabrics should have less contrast within the fabric itself. It can still be a print, but smaller and with less color variation. The furthest pieces should be solid or at least faint, monochromatic with little value variation, prints.

You can use ghosting in various ways. In *Phantom Square Dance* (page 80) and *Hopscotch* (page 84), ghosting provides duplicate images — almost like the "floaters" you see when you look at something bright and then look away. In *Shadow Boxing* (page 90), the ghost images influence how your eye moves across the design, it defines a path.

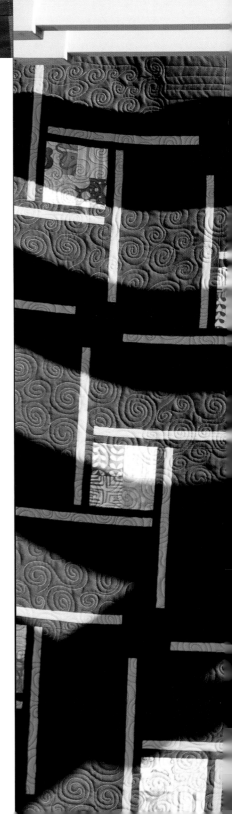

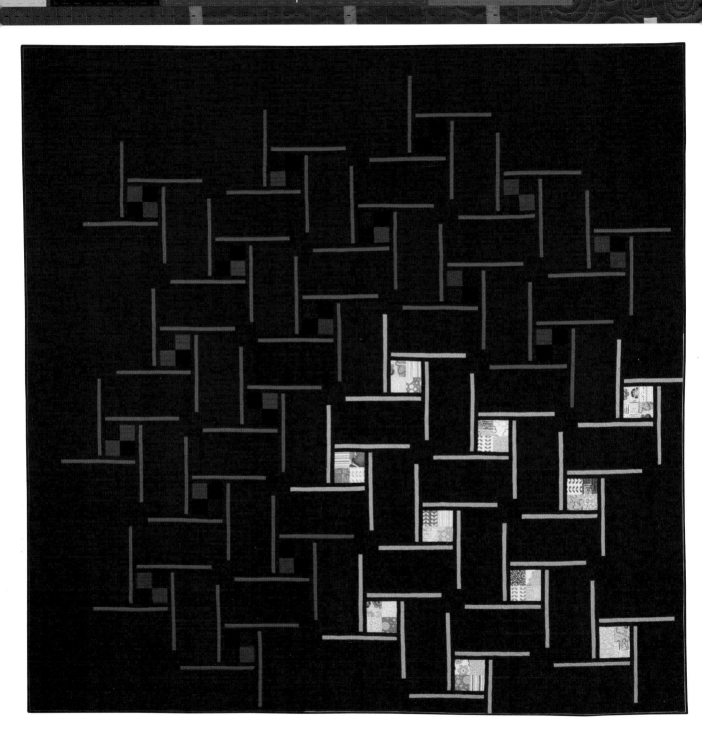

The prominent design of *Phantom Square Dance* is in the lower right corner. The fabrics in the four-patches are bright and lively. The lines surrounding them are pure and bright. Against the dark background, this area is the focal point of the quilt. I could have left the design at that. Then the quilting in the negative space would become the next design element and could have added the necessary design.

I wanted this quilt to have more depth than that. To make this happen, I continued the design to cover the majority of the quilt, but made the other blocks blend into the background — kind of like ghosts! To do this, I chose fabrics that were solid and dark. The quilting becomes the third layer of design. Although it provides some impact, it's not as impactful as the pieced design of the negative space.

To make this quilt successful, it's important that the ghosted area is subtle. Those pieces must blend with the background. So, if you are using a light background, the ghost fabrics will be lighter and the positive design space will use bright fabrics. In this case, I used a dark background with dark ghost fabrics and light fabric in the positive space.

### *Phantom Square* Dance Fabric Details

At QuiltCon 2013, Moda was giving away mini-charm packs: 2½" charm squares. The mini-charm pack that I got was from the Ticklish line. When I returned home, I put this set aside and tried to figure out how I could use this small pack of fabric to make a large quilt. This quilt is the result of that personal challenge. The solids are Kona cottons: raisin (my favorite neutrally purple), peacock, glacier, avocado, regal, marine.

## FABRIC REQUIREMENTS

1 mini charm pack (at least 40 — 2½" squares) or 10 — 5" charm squares cut into 4 — 2½" squares for the prominent four-patch blocks

¼ yard each of 3 different dark solids for the ghosted four-patch blocks

½ yard bright aqua for the lines in the prominent design area

¾ yard dark aqua for the lines in the ghosted area

6¾ yards dark background

## CUTTING

### DARK SOLIDS
2 strips 2½" x wof of each dark solid
Crosscut to get 23 — 2½" squares (69 total, 68 are needed).

### BRIGHT AQUA
1 strip 10½" x wof

### DARK AQUA
2 strips 10½" x wof

## BACKGROUND

3 strips 2" x wof — set aside

1 strip 8" x wof

Crosscut the 8" strip:

- 2 — 7" x 8" rectangles
- 1 — 6" x 8" rectangle
- 1 — 2½" x 8" rectangle
- 1 — 3" x 8" rectangle
- 1 — 8½" x 7" rectangle

17 strips 12" x wof

Crosscut 7 of the 12" strips into 41 — 6" x 12" rectangles.

Crosscut 2 of the 12" strips into 7 — 7" x 12" rectangles.

Crosscut 3 of the 12" strips into 108 — 1" x 12" rectangles.

Crosscut the remaining 5 — 12" strips:

- Strip 1: 24½", 14"
- Strip 2: 17½", 13½", 9"
- Strip 3: 17", 12½", 7½", 3"
- Strip 4: 2 — 6½", 13", 10½", 3½"
- Strip 5: 11", 16½", 9½"

From the leftover pieces, cut 1 — 7 x 11½" and 1 — 13½" x 11".

With a remaining piece, cut a 6½" x 15" background strip.

## PIECING

Using the bright 2½" squares, make 10 four-patch blocks.

Using the dark, solid squares, make 17 four-patch blocks.

Attach the bright aqua strip to 1 of the 2" background strips. Press the seam to the darkest fabric. Cut into 40 — 1" pieces.

Repeat with the 2 dark aqua strips. Cut into 68 — 1" pieces.

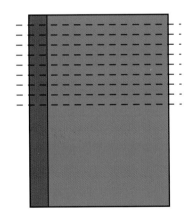

Using the aqua pieces, the 1" x 12" background, and the 6" x 12" background rectangles, piece the blocks as shown. Make:

- 12 blocks using all bright aqua
- 7 blocks using 1 bright aqua and 1 dark aqua piece
- 22 blocks using all dark aqua

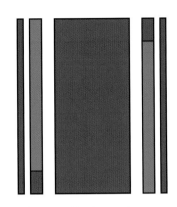

Using the 7" x 12" background pieces, aqua pieces, and 1" x 12" background pieces, piece the blocks as shown. Make:

- 3 blocks using bright aqua
- 4 blocks using dark aqua

Piece all of the perimeter blocks according to the diagram. They are all pieced in the same manner as the previous block, but the large background size will vary.

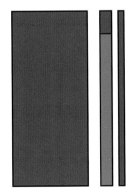

Note on the diagram: dark aqua strips are attached to 11" x 7" backgrounds, bright aqua strips are attached to 7" x 8" and 7" x 8½" backgrounds (they will be trimmed to fit).

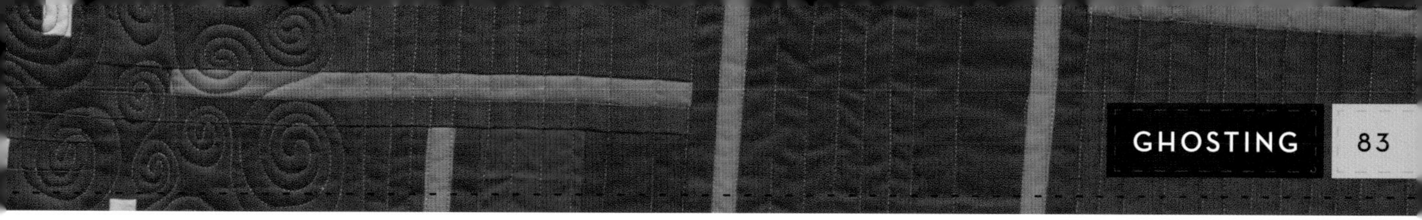



## ASSEMBLY

Continue to piece the quilt according to the diagram. Use partial seams (see General Instructions, page 12) as indicated at the circles.

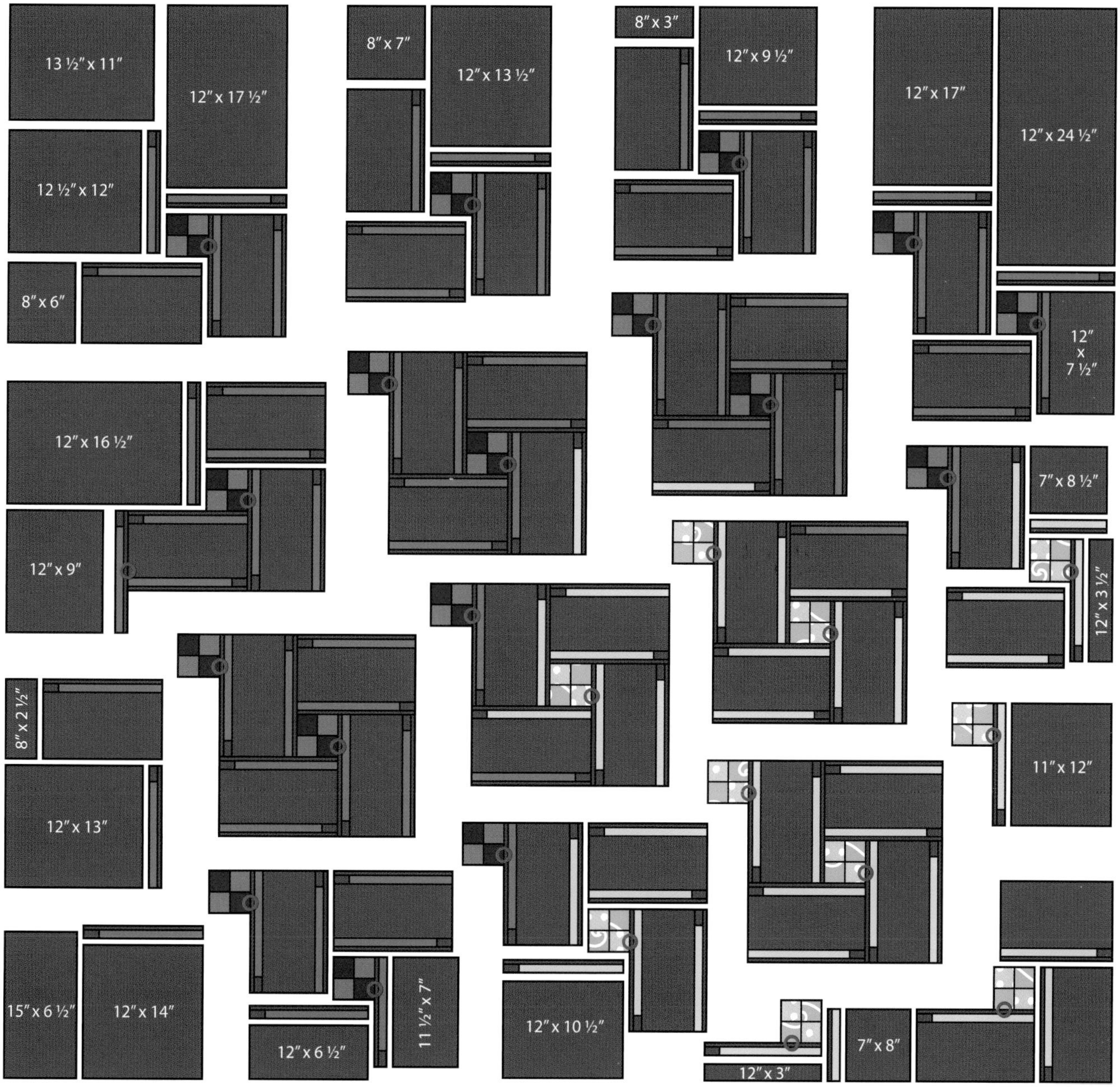
13 ½″ x 11″
12″ x 17 ½″
12 ½″ x 12″
8″ x 6″
8″ x 7″
12″ x 13 ½″
8″ x 3″
12″ x 9 ½″
12″ x 17″
12″ x 24 ½″
12″ x 7 ½″
12″ x 16 ½″
12″ x 9″
7″ x 8 ½″
12″ x 3 ½″
8″ x 2 ½″
12″ x 13″
11″ x 12″
15″ x 6 ½″
12″ x 14″
12″ x 6 ½″
11 ½″ x 7″
12″ x 10 ½″
7″ x 8″
12″ x 3″

ASSEMBLY DIAGRAM

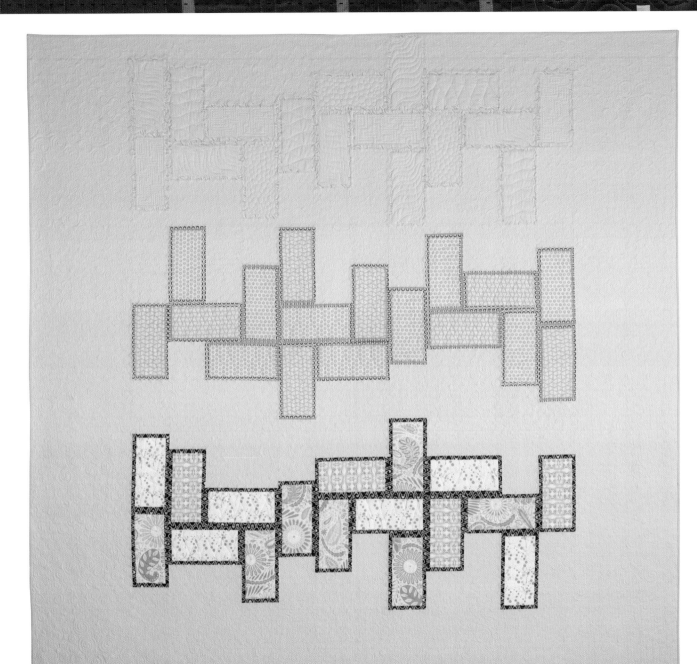

*Hopscotch* is a simple quilt with a lot of impact. It is perfect if you have three or four large, bold prints you want to showcase. That's exactly how this design came to fruition. It started with one fabric that I wanted to highlight. I found a couple of more bold prints to go along with it. To make each print stand on its own, each is framed with a small, dark border.

The boxes fit together like a puzzle to make one large rectangle. That could have been the entire design: a rectangle of design across the bottom, with a lot of fabric to fill the negative space. If this is what I had sent to a quilter, I can imagine that the quilting would have mimicked the rectangles in the negative space.

I continued piecing into the negative space. I made the same design, this time using fabrics with a smaller scale print, less variation in the colors, and in the same general color range as the background. This variation is also framed, but this time using a fabric color that is somewhere between the background and the first framing fabric.

I wanted the final set to be barely noticeable. These frames are just a shade darker than the background. Only one print is used in the rectangles: a monochromatic print the same shade as the background.

## *Hopscotch* Fabric Details

Another QuiltCon 2013 inspired quilt! This one started at the Spoonflower booth with a spinning wheel game. I won a free fat-quarter of my design. At home, of course I got it out the day before the offer expired! I hurried to design a grown-up ballet fabric, inspired by my daughter, a dancer whose favorite colors are aqua and green. I designed this quilt to showcase this fabric — I didn't want to cut it up too much. The other large print was from my stash. The other prints are mostly from Art Gallery's Carnaby Street collection. The small border in the lightest section was pulled from my stash — I remember buying it about 18 years ago! The solid is Kona aqua.

## FABRIC REQUIREMENTS

4¼ yards light aqua for background
Prints needed:
    Bottom design — high contrast
    Middle design — low to medium contrast
    Top design — minimal contrast
Large rectangles: ¾ yard total for each design
Small borders: ½ yard for each design

## CUTTING

### BACKGROUND

Cut 3 — 10½" strips across the width of fabric. Unfold and stack the 3 strips, then cut a total of:

- 3 — 9½"
- 3 — 6½"
- 12 — 5½"

Cut 5 — 5½" strips across the width.

Unfold and stack 3 of the strips then cut a total of:

- 3 — 20½"
- 9 — 5½"
- 3 — 4½"
- 3 — 1½"

Unfold and stack the remaining 2 strips then cut a total of:

- 2 — 8½"
- 2 — 7½"
- 2 — 2½"
- 2 — 3½"

Separate the remaining uncut portion of the strips and cut:

- 1 — 8½"
- 1 — 7½"
- 1 — 2½"
- 1 — 3½"

Using the remaining yardage, cut borders the length of the fabric:

- 2 — 13½" x 75½"
- 1 — 13½" x 86½"

### FOREGROUND

Cut the large rectangles for each design of fabric:

- 17 — 4½" x 9½" (for each design)

Cut the small borders for each design of fabric:

- 13 — 1" strips the width of the fabric.

From 8 of the strips cut:

- 4 — 1" x 5½" (for each strip)
- 2 — 1" x 9½" (for each strip)

From 4 of the strips cut:

- 4 — 1" x 9½" (for each strip)

From the 1 remaining strip cut:

- 2 — 1" x 5½"
- 2 — 1" x 9½"

## PIECING

**Make 17 of these blocks for each design.**

For each design, border each rectangle with the small border fabric.

Add the border to the long sides of each rectangle. Press with the seam toward the border.

Add the border to the short sides of each rectangle. Press with the seam toward the border.

## ASSEMBLY

Assemble the resulting blocks like this for each design:

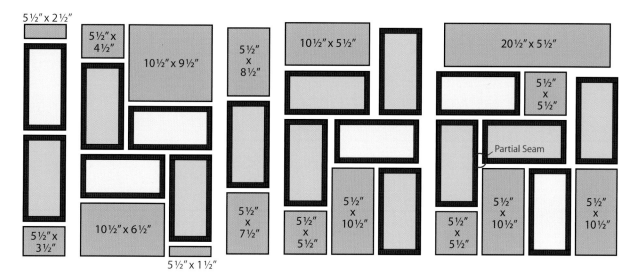

At this point, you will have 3 large pieced sections. Turn the middle section upside down. Piece these 3 sections together, press. Add the 2 side borders, press. Attach the bottom border, press.

The individual panels are 20½" x 25½".

The finished panels are 60½" x 25½".

ASSEMBLY DIAGRAM

## QUILTING

When Tammy Lawson saw this quilt, she knew instantly how she would quilt it. She wanted to fill the negative space with spirals — lots of them! She planned to use 3–4 different fillers for each of the rectangles, but chose to only use those on the top row. She ended up using a simple quilt design for the second and third rows as she didn't want to take away from the prints. She enjoyed bringing this quilt to life and even applied the binding for me!

Tammy is a longarm quilter — she quilts for others as well as herself. She loves teaching her craft to others, especially to any of her grandchildren who show an interest. She also enjoys quilting for Quilts of Valor and local cancer research charity quilts. Tammy is the owner of Quiltin' Kaboodle and lives in Indianapolis, IN. You can see more of her work at www.quiltinkaboodle.com.

*Shadow Boxing* is another quilt that highlights a large, bright print. Three brightly framed prints are the focal point of this quilt — they are positioned so your eye moves across the quilt. Using two different colors for these frames helps the design by adding depth. If they were all framed the same, this part of the design would fall pretty flat. I added ghost frames to strengthen the path that your eye would naturally follow from one bright frame to the next. For a more subtle look, use smaller, monochromatic prints for the ghost images or make them solid. I felt that these prints could stand up to the busy owl print.

Three shapes (far right and bottom left) feature bright prints. "Ghost" images are done in dull solids. The background is dark.

## *Shadow Boxing* Fabric Details

I had a general design in mind when I went hunting for a large scale, fun print. I settled on Michael Miller's Swedish Owl print. The brown background, orange and blue frames are all Kona cottons selected based on the colors in the owl print. Then I came across the tree-inspired Stella prints. They are a little brighter than I was looking for, but I love the theme. The brown borders of the smaller frames are Moda crossweaves from my stash.

## FABRIC REQUIREMENTS

½–¾ yard focus fabric (½ yard if print runs across the bolt; ¾ yard if print runs down the bolt)

¼ yard ghost print #1

¼ yard ghost print #2

½ yard aqua solid (large frame)

¼ yard orange solid (small focus frames)

½ yard medium brown (ghost frames)

¼ yard dark brown (ghost frames)

3½ yards dark brown background print

## CUTTING

Cut the blocks at differing angles. All of these sizes are approximate due to the odd angles. As the strips are cut, pair them with the fabric squares as noted to prepare for the piecing.

### FOCUS FABRIC

3 wonky squares approximately:

- 16" x 22"
- 6" x 8"
- 4" x 7"

### GHOST PRINT #1

3 wonky squares approximately:

- 10" x 13"
- 5" x 8"
- 4" x 6"

## GHOST PRINT #2

2 wonky squares approximately:

- 6" x 8"
- 5" x 6"

## AQUA (LARGE FRAME)

pair with the large focus fabric square:

- 2 strips 5" x 18"
- 2 strips 5" x 36"

## ORANGE (SMALL FOCUS FRAMES)

pair with the medium focus fabric square:

- 2 strips 3½" x 8"
- 2 strips 3½" x 16"

pair with the small focus fabric square:

- 2 strips 2½" x 5"
- 2 strips 2½" x 12"

## MEDIUM BROWN (GHOST FRAMES)

pair with the large square of print #1:

- 2 strips 3" x 12"
- 2 strips 3" x 20"

pair with the medium square of print #1:

- 2 strips 2" x 10"
- 2 strips 2" x 14"

pair with the small square of print #1:

- 2 strips 2½" x 6"
- 2 strips 2½" x 14"

## DARK BROWN (GHOST FRAMES)

pair with the large square of print #2:

- 2 strips 2½" x 8"
- 2 strips 2½" x 15"

pair with the small square of print #2:

- 2 strips 2" x 7"
- 2 strips 2" x 12"

## BACKGROUND FABRIC

See piecing instructions.

## PIECING

For each of the squares cut, attach the paired frames. Attach the shortest strips to the top and bottom of the squares. Press and trim. Attach the longer strips to each side. Press.

Trim each framed square at odd angles.

## ASSEMBLY

Lay out the squares in the general fashion of the diagram at right.

Trace where the top frame overlaps the bottom frame with chalk shown with the blue line below.

Cut ½" from the dashed line shown below toward the overlap to create a seam allowance.

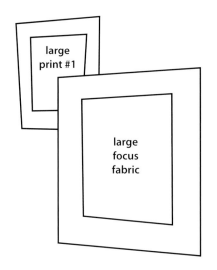

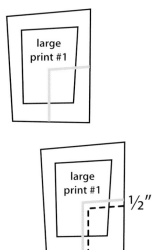

small
focus
fabric

small
print #2

small
print #1

large
print #1

large
print #2

large
focus
fabric

medium
print #1

medium
focus
fabric

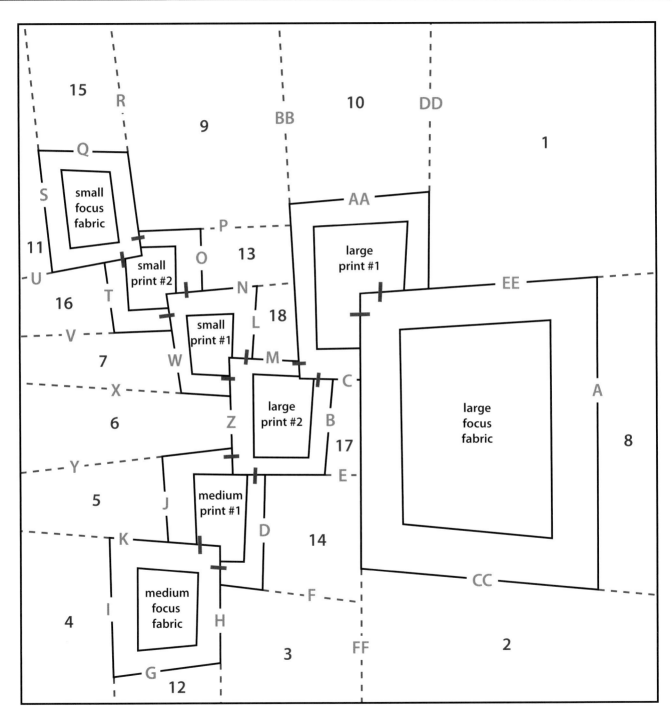

ASSEMBLY DIAGRAM — NUMBERS INDICATE CUTTING ORDER, LETTERS INDICATE PIECING ORDER
NOTE: DOUBLE LETTERS (AA, BB) FOLLOW Z.

Cut the background fabric. For the most efficient use of the fabric, cut the largest areas first (the diagram shows the largest to smallest pieces). Measure the area and cut a generous piece to cover the spaces — the fabric should have a 2" margin on each side. The cutting shouldn't be accurate nor should the angles be taken into consideration at this time.

Constructing the top is a process of making one section, then adding an adjoining section. In general, the steps are:

- Chalk the overlap.
- Cut the seam allowance ½" from the chalk line, away from the center of the fabric.
- Stitch the seam.
- Press.

To begin, take piece #8. Place it under the edge of the large focus frame (seam A). With the help of a ruler, chalk a line along the raw edge of the frame. Move the background piece to a cutting surface. Cut ½" from the chalk line (away from the center of the fabric — to extend the seam allowance). Stitch seam A.

Move on to piece #17. Mark seam B, leaving plenty of fabric extending beyond the adjacent seams. Stitch and press. Put it back in place and mark seam C. Mark and cut the seam allowance. Start the stitching about 2" from the inside corner (as indicated in the diagram). Be sure to lock the stitch at the start. When pressing, press the entire seam, including the corner that hasn't been stitched (to prepare for hand-stitching at the end).

Continue piecing in the order indicated. Numbers indicate cutting order (largest pieces first), the letters indicate piecing order.

Once all the piecing is complete, turn under and hand stitch the loose corners in place with a running or whip stitch.

## QUILTING

Stephanie Dodson was immediately drawn to *Shadow Boxing*. Both the composition and fabric choice inspired organic quilting to help tell the story of the quilt. She mimicked the scribbles in one of the fabrics to frame the focus fabrics, with the circular stitching creating an interesting contrast to the pronounced angles of the blocks. Tone-on-tone leaves in the negative space were a natural fit for the whimsical owls and tree branch fabric. To add visual depth, Stephanie stitched a subtle ninth "block," repeating the shape and quilting of the other cascading blocks.

Stephanie is a fiber artist and graphic designer in the Kansas City metropolitan area. She and her husband, Doug, an Army veteran, own Summerwind Studio LLC. As part of the longarm quilting component of their business, they are active supporters of Quilts of Valor. Learn more at www.summerwindstudio.com.

# PIECING

Piecing the negative space is very versatile. It can add depth to the negative space but it can also be used to reinforce a story that your quilt is trying to convey. Any piecing method will work. As always, subtlety is paramount. Piecing can be simple or it can be intricate, but keep the fabrics all in the same color family — analogous colors, low contrast in values. The goal is to have the primary design be the most impactful. Those who look more closely will be rewarded by subtleties in the background piecing that isn't evident at first glance.

*Distorted Justice* (page 98) gets its name from the negative space piecing of Courthouse Steps blocks. Without the background piecing, this quilt would be nice, but pretty flat. In *Savanna Nights* (page 102), the negative space piecing takes the African animals from the improv blocks and puts them on a Savanna. You can almost feel the arid night. *Mod Roses* (page 108), features the negative space, filled with rose vines, to evoke the feeling of a garden.

The improv blocks in this quilt are pieced in the same way as the traditional Courthouse Steps block, but with improvisational cutting. When it came to filling in the negative space, I wanted to pay homage to the traditional block that inspired the piecing. The traditional blocks are pieced into the background, using all cream and white fabrics with very little color variation. That's still a lot of white space, so every now and then, I added a small little wedge of color — a very subtle, light steel blue.

### *Distorted Justice* Fabric Details

This quilt was made for Michael Miller's 2013 Madrona Road fabric challenge. The prints are all from this fabric line. The yellow-gold solid is Michael Miller's Cotton Couture in straw. The rest of the solids are Kona cotton.

## FABRIC REQUIREMENTS

1½ yards of light cream for background

Fat eighths of 3–4 different whites and creams for the courthouse square blocks

4–5 fat quarters of large contrasting scraps for the blocks

## CUTTING

Cut 1½" to 2" strips from the creams and whites for Courthouse Steps blocks. The other blocks are improv pieced.

## PIECING

Other than the Courthouse Steps blocks, all piecing is done using gentle curves. Cut the curves by placing one piece, right side up, on a cutting mat. Place the adjacent piece on top, right side up, with just enough overlap to accommodate the curve. With a rotary cutter, cut a gentle curve. Piece, using a seam allowance a little less than ¼", and press to one side.

When adding background pieces, cut in small strips of a slightly contrasting fabric every now and then.

## COURTHOUSE STEPS BLOCKS

Use the cream and white strips. Start with a square center cut from 1 of the strips. Add strips to each side of the center. Trim. Press. Add strips to the top and bottom. Trim. Press. Continue adding strips until you have 3 blocks that measure approximately: 9½" square, 7½" square, and 6" square.

## IMPROV BLOCKS

Note: Refer to the Assembly Diagram on page 101. Many seams are curve pieced.

### BLOCK 1

Start with a center about 3½" x 5".

Cut strips of a different print about 1½" wide.

Add strips until all 4 sides are bordered.

Add a thin strip of contrasting fabric to the left side of the block.

Frame the block with background fabric to get a 16½" x 9" rectangle, with about 5½" of background to the right and 7½" to the left.

### BLOCK 2

Start with a center about 4½" x 5".

Cut a strip of fabric about 1" wide. Add this to the top and left side.

Cut a strip of another fabric about 1½" wide. Add to the right and bottom.

Add a piece of background fabric (about 1½" wide) to the left side.

Using the print from the top, add a 1½" strip across the bottom.

Continue adding background fabric to make the block measure 9½" x 11".

### BLOCK 3

Start with a center about 3" x 6".

Add a 1" print strip, then a 2½" background strip to the right side.

Add a 1" print strip to the top. Add 6" x 5" background piece to the top.

Add a 1½" print strip, then a different 1½" print to the left side.

Add a 4½" background strip to the left side.

Add a 1" print strip across the bottom.

Continue filling out with background fabric to make an 18" x 11" block.

### BLOCK 4

Start with a center about 5½" x 8½".

Add 1" print strips to the right side and the top.

# Distorted Justice

Add a 2" background strip to the right side.

Add a 3" background strip to the top.

Add a 1" print strip to the left side and bottom.

Add a different 1" print strip to the left.

Cut a 1" print strip and trim so it is a couple of inches shorter than the bottom.

Add a background piece to make the strip longer and attach to the bottom.

This block should measure about 9½" x 12".

## BLOCK 5

Start with a center about 3" x 4".

Add a 1" print strip, then a 3½" piece of background to the right.

Add a 1½" print strip to the left side.

Add a 1" print strip across the top cutting it so the curve runs off soon after the right hand print strip.

Add a 1" print strip, then a 1½" background strip to the bottom.

This block should measure about 6½" x 9½".

## BLOCK 6

Start with a center about 4" x 4".

Add a 1" print strip across the top.

Add a 1" strip of a different print to the bottom, left and top.

Add 2" background to the bottom and 1½" piece to the top.

Add a 1" print strip to the right.

Fill with background to get an 8½" x 19½" block.

## ASSEMBLY

Attach Block 1 to the 9½" Courthouse Steps to make the top row.

Attach Block 2 to Block 3 to make the second row.

To the 7½" Courthouse Steps block, add 2½" background to the top; 3" to the right; 10½" to the bottom. Attach this to the right side of block 6. This makes the bottom left corner.

To the 6" Courthouse Steps block, add 2" background to the left and 1½" to the right. Attach Block 4 to the top of the Courthouse Steps and Block 5 to the bottom. This makes the bottom right corner.

Attach the 2 bottom corners making the third row.

Attach the 3 rows.

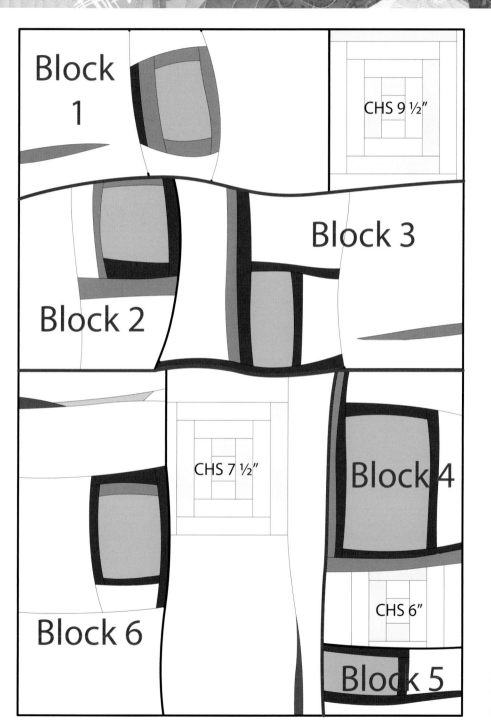

Block 1

CHS 9 ½"

ROW 1

Block 3

Block 2

ROW 2

CHS 7 ½"

Block 4

ROW 3

CHS 6"

Block 6

Block 5

ASSEMBLY
DIAGRAM — RED
LINES INDICATE
FINAL 4 SEAMS.

*Savanna Nights* was inspired by a print depicting African animals. I love the playfulness of the improvisational blocks. Although I do like to piece improvisationally, I usually do so with an overall plan. In this case, I wanted to be able to set the four blocks together and have them relate. That's why I chose to have them come together and form a star-like shape of yellow with a darker border of purple. An entire quilt made of these blocks might have been too much, but they are perfect for one section. I wanted to reinforce the idea of the African Savanna. The Acacia tree is indicative of the landscape — I think when most people see this shape, they think of the savanna. So rather than just put these animals in the corner of a quilt, I wanted to put them into a savanna setting.

### *Savanna Nights* Fabric Details

The fabric that inspired this quilt is an Echino print. The fabric used in the improv piecing was all from my scrap bins. The other solids are In The Beginning Modern Solids — crossweaves that are a very nice weight to work with.

## FABRIC REQUIREMENTS

Focal print — whatever is needed to get 4 images
Scraps for improvisational piecing in yellow, orange, pink, purple
¾ yard teal for tree top
1 yard darker blue for borders and tree trunk
2¾ yards blue for background

## CUTTING

### FOCAL PRINT
Cut 4 images.

### TEAL
Cut 12 —1½" strips.
Crosscut the strips as indicated in the Tree Top Piecing Instructions. Piece strips together to get the longer cuts.

### DARK BLUE
Cut 2 — 1½" strips.
- Crosscut the strips as indicated in the Tree Top Piecing Instructions.
Cut 2 — 5½" strips.
- Crosscut as indicated in the Blocks Piecing Instructions.
Cut 2 — 4½" strips.
- Crosscut as indicated in the Blocks Piecing Instructions.
Cut 3 — 2" strips.
- Crosscut as indicated in the Blocks Piecing Instructions.

## BLUE BACKGROUND

Cut according to the diagram (right). From the remaining blue background, cut 4 — 1" strips.

- Crosscut 8 — 20½" pieces (to use in Tree Trunk).

Cut 11 — 1½" strips.

- Crosscut according to the Tree Top and Tree Trunk diagrams (see next page).

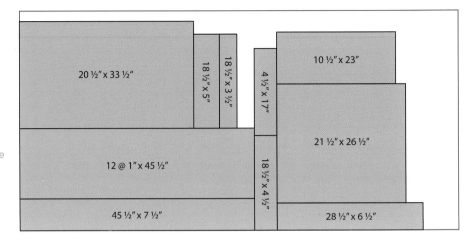

## PIECING

### BLOCKS

Make 4 improvisationally pieced blocks using the focal print as the center. Plan the piecing so the inner corner is in the yellow range, and the outer edges are dark. Continue to piece each block until they can be trimmed to the indicated sizes.

Frame each block as indicated.

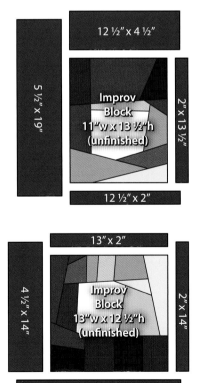

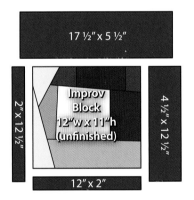

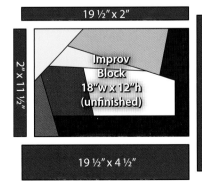

## TREE TOP

Piece each row as indicated. Stitch the rows together with a 1" x 45½" background strip between each row.

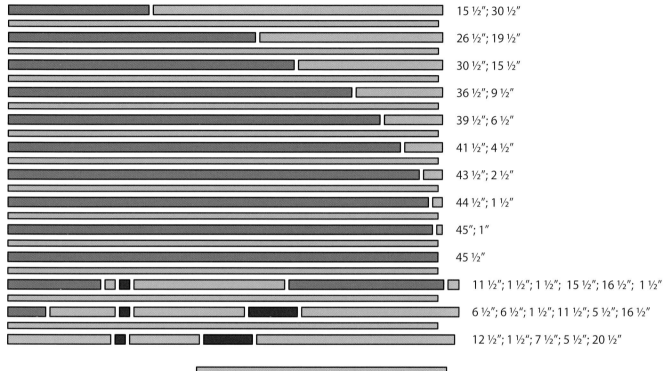

15 ½"; 30 ½"

26 ½"; 19 ½"

30 ½"; 15 ½"

36 ½"; 9 ½"

39 ½"; 6 ½"

41 ½"; 4 ½"

43 ½"; 2 ½"

44 ½"; 1 ½"

45"; 1"

45 ½"

11 ½"; 1 ½"; 1 ½"; 15 ½"; 16 ½"; 1 ½"

6 ½"; 6 ½"; 1 ½"; 11 ½"; 5 ½"; 16 ½"

12 ½"; 1 ½"; 7 ½"; 5 ½"; 20 ½"

## TREE TRUNK

Piece each row as indicated. Stitch the rows together with a 1" x 20½" background strip between each row.

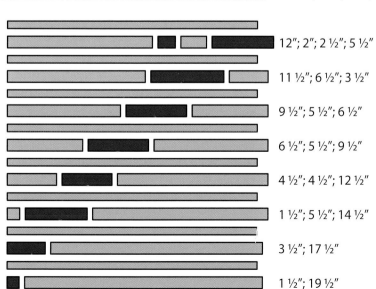

12"; 2"; 2 ½"; 5 ½"

11 ½"; 6 ½"; 3 ½"

9 ½"; 5 ½"; 6 ½"

6 ½"; 5 ½"; 9 ½"

4 ½"; 4 ½"; 12 ½"

1 ½"; 5 ½"; 14 ½"

3 ½"; 17 ½"

1 ½"; 19 ½"

## ASSEMBLY

Piece all of the sections together as indicated at right.

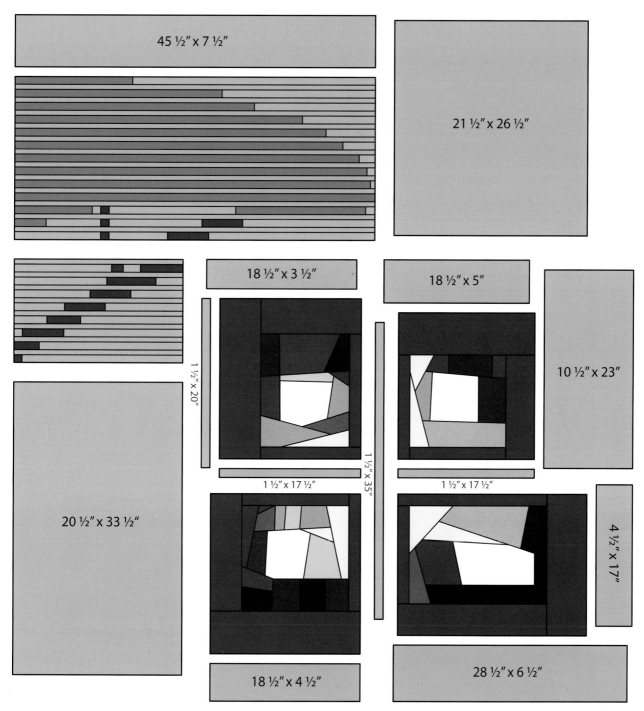

ASSEMBLY DIAGRAM

*Mod Roses* was designed around a set of improv rose blocks. The leaf blocks were added to give some grounding to the roses — otherwise, I think they would appear to be floating around. The negative space incorporates the vines (the thorns were added in the quilting) to evoke the feeling of being in a garden — rather than flowers in a vase.

You can use the vines to your advantage by planning the pathways your eye can follow. I usually like quilt movement from upper left to lower right, then circle over to the left and then to the middle right, so I find that that influences my design. In this case, the vines lead in from the upper left and flow through to the lower right. The series of leaf blocks at the bottom bring the eye back to the left and the vines draw the eye over to the top rose block. At least that's how I see it!

## *Mod Roses* Fabric Details

The fabric used to make the roses was from my scrap bins and my stash. I pulled anything I could find in the pink to orange range. The greens are all Kona cottons: tarragon, peridot, avocado.

## FABRIC REQUIREMENTS

Scraps of pink and orange prints for roses
1 yard dark green for leaves, frames and
    binding
¾ yard medium green for stems (just a little
    darker than the background)
3¼ yards light green for background

## SUPPLIES

Starch
1" bias tape maker

## CUTTING

### DARK GREEN FRAMES
6 — 2" strips x wof
6 — 1" strips x wof

### MEDIUM GREEN STEMS
1¾" wide bias cut strips totaling 190" in length

### LIGHT GREEN BACKGROUND
Cut across the width: 61", 14", 7½", 4½", the leftover is for the improvisational piecing.

*See cutting diagram on the next page.*

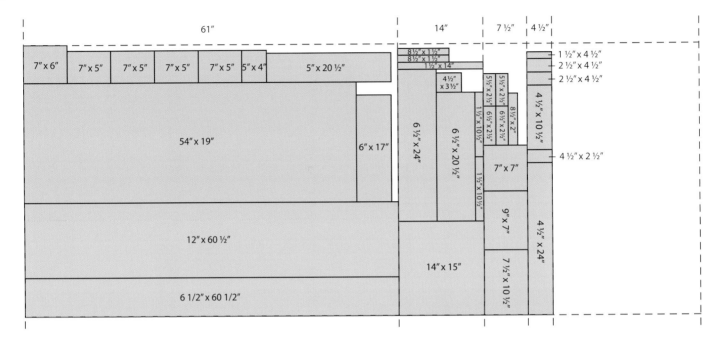

| | 61" | | 14" | 7 ½" | 4 ½" |

7" x 6"   7" x 5"   7" x 5"   7" x 5"   7" x 5"   5" x 4"   5" x 20 ½"

8 ½" x 1 ½"
8 ½" x 1 ½"
1 ½" x 14"
1 ½" x 4 ½"
2 ½" x 4 ½"
2 ½" x 4 ½"

4 ½" x 3 ½"

54" x 19"

6" x 17"

6 ½" x 24"   6 ½" x 20 ½"   5 ½" x 2 ½"   1 ½" x 10 ½"   6 ½" x 2 ½"   8 ½" x 2"   4 ½" x 10 ½"

4 ½" x 2 ½"

7" x 7"

1 ½" x 10 ½"

9" x 7"

4 ½" x 24"

12" x 60 ½"

14" x 15"

7 ½" x 10 ½"

6 1/2" x 60 1/2"

## PIECING

The key to piecing the leaves and roses is to cut shallow curves.

## LEAVES

Cut the background for each leaf block large. Each will be trimmed to the correct size after it is pieced.

Cut a dark green leaf shape about the size of the finished block. Place it on top of the background piece (right sides up). Cut along 1 side of the leaf. Pull the cut piece away from the leaf. Cut the other side. Piece it in the opposite order of cutting. Place the last background piece and the leaf right sides together. Stitch with a small seam allowance (less than ¼"). Press. Repeat with the other side. Trim to the final size (see table).

Frame each block with 1" wide dark green strips. Attach the strips to the sides of the block. Press. Trim. Repeat with the top and bottom.

| Leaves Needed | | |
|---|---|---|
| Cut Size | Trim To | Orientation |
| 9" x 7" | 7½" x 5½" | |
| 7" x 5" | 5½" x 3½" | |
| 5" x 4" | 3½" x 2½" | |
| 7" x 7" | 5½" x 5½" | |
| 7" x 6" | 5½" x 4½" | |
| 7" x 5" | 5½" x 3½" | |
| 7" x 5" | 5½" x 3½" | |
| 7" x 5" | 5½" x 3½" | |

## ROSES

Cut a rudimentary circle to be the center of the rose. The circle should have about 5 squared off sides.

Add petals 1 at a time. Lay the petal fabric down — right side up. Place the circle on top (also right side up), overlapping the side where the petal will be attached. Cut the petal fabric following the contour of the circle. Put the right sides together and piece with a small seam allowance (a little less than ¼"). Press. Trim the petal to be a little larger than the final size.

Continue adding petals in the same manner.

When the flower is the size that you want, add leaves. Determine the width of the background fabric needed to get the rose to the final size. Cut a piece of background about 2" larger. Cut a leaf shape from dark green. Place the leaf on top of the background and cut 1 side of the light green along the contour of the leaf. Put right sides together, piece, press, and trim. Place that piece on top of the remaining background piece. Again, cut along the contour of the leaf. Repeat the same steps.

Make as many leaves as you'd like for the rose. Fill in the background of the rose in the same manner as adding petals. Use the leaf pieces and solid background pieces. Continue to add background pieces until you get to the necessary size.

Starch the block and press. Because the block will be left with a lot of outside bias edges, the block should be heavily starched. Trim to the correct size:

- Large Rose: 15½" x 21"

- Medium Rose: 15" x 17½"

- Small Rose: 11" x 15"

Frame the block with 2" dark green strips. Attach strips to the top and bottom of the block. Press. Trim. Repeat with the sides.

## ASSEMBLY

Piece the quilt according to the Assembly Diagram on the next page.

### STEMS

Join the medium green bias strips with a 45° seam (as you would to make binding). Press the seam open. Cut 1 end at a sharp angle. Feed this end into the bias tape maker. Spray starch onto the next 2–3 feet of strips that will feed through the bias tape maker. With a hot iron against the end of the bias tape maker, pull the tape maker as you move the iron down the length of the fabric.

Lay the stems over the background however you would like. Pin them in place. When the stem meets a seam, open the seam with a seam ripper, making a gap just wide enough to insert the stem. Pull the stem through the opening ensuring that the stem lies flat. Re-stitch the seam. Appliqué the stems in place.

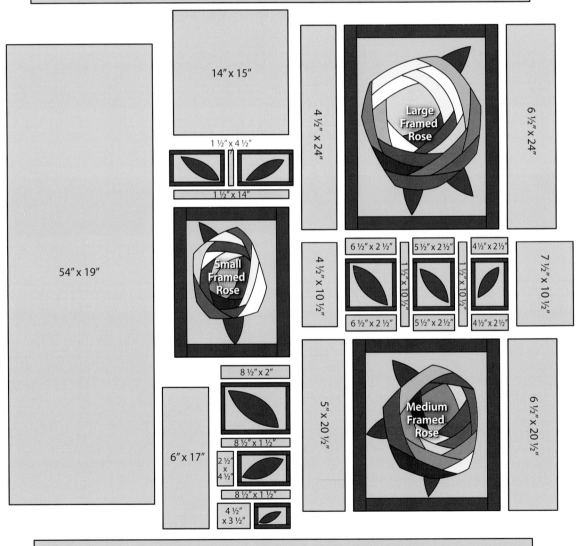

12" x 60 ½"

14" x 15"

4 ½" x 24"

Large Framed Rose

6 ½" x 24"

54" x 19"

1 ½" x 4 ½"

1 ½" x 14"

Small Framed Rose

6 ½" x 2 ½"   5 ½" x 2 ½"   4 ½" x 2 ½"

4 ½" x 10 ½"   1 ½" x 10 ½"   1 ½" x 10 ½"   7 ½" x 10 ½"

6 ½" x 2 ½"   5 ½" x 2 ½"   4 ½" x 2 ½"

8 ½" x 2"

6" x 17"

8 ½" x 1 ½"

5" x 20 ½"

Medium Framed Rose

6 ½" x 20 ½"

2 ½" x 4 ½"

8 ½" x 1 ½"

4 ½" x 3 ½"

6 ½" x 60 ½"

ASSEMBLY DIAGRAM